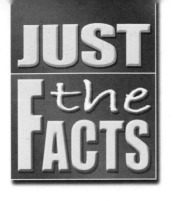

HUMAN
BODY

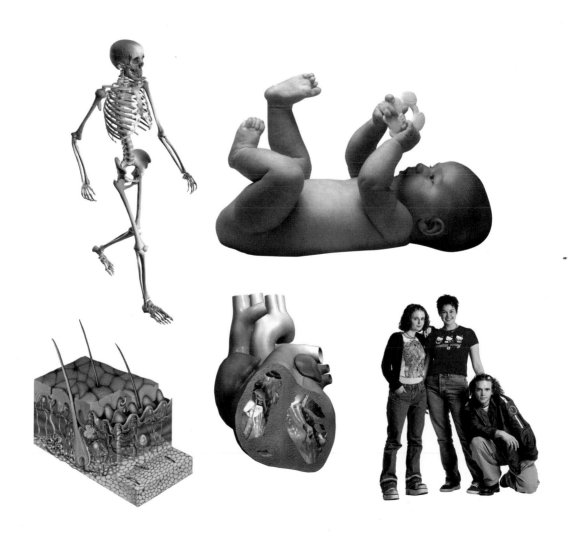

This edition published in the United States in 2006 by School Specialty Publishing, a member of the School Specialty Family.
Copyright © ticktock Entertainment Ltd 2005 First published in Great Britain in 2005 by ticktock Media Ltd. Printed in China.

Written by Steve Parker.

Library of Congress-in-Publication Data is on file with the publisher.

Send all inquiries to:
School Specialty Publishing
8720 Orion Place
Columbus, OH 43240-2111

ISBN 0-7696- 4255-1
1 2 3 4 5 6 7 8 9 10 TTM 11 10 09 08 07 06

CONTENTS

HOW TO USE THIS BOOK

JUST THE FACTS, HUMAN BODY is a quick and easy-to-use way to look up facts about the systems that control how our bodies work. Every page is packed with cut-away diagrams, charts, scientific terms and key pieces of information. For fast access to just the facts, follow the tips on these pages.

WHERE IN THE BODY?
An at-a-glance look at where the part of the body can be found.

INTRODUCTION TO TOPIC

TWO QUICK WAYS TO FIND A FACT:

1 Look at the detailed **CONTENTS** list on page 3 to find your topic of interest.

Turn to the relevant page and use the **BOX HEADINGS** to find the information box you need.

2 Turn to the **INDEX** that starts on page 60 and search for key words relating to your research.
• The index will direct you to the correct page, and where on the page to find the fact you need.

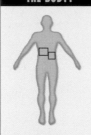

WHERE IN THE BODY?

The liver is in the upper abdomen, behind the lower right ribs. The pancreas is in the upper left abdomen, behind the stomach.

LIVER AND PANCREAS

The body can't digest food with just its digestive tract. The body also needs the liver and pancreas. These are next to the stomach and they are digestive glands, which means they make powerful substances to break down food in the intestines. Together with the digestive tract, the liver and pancreas make up the whole digestive system.

WARM LIVER

The liver is so busy with chemical processes and tasks that it makes lots of heat.

• When the body is at rest and the muscles are still, the liver makes up to one-fifth of the body's total warmth.

• The heat from the liver isn't wasted. Blood spreads the heat all around the body.

See pages 34–35 for information on the CIRCULATORY SYSTEM.

GALL BLADDER AND BILE

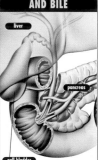

liver

pancreas

gall bladder

The gall bladder is a small storage bag under the liver.

• It is 3.1 in. long and 1.1in. wide.

• Some of the bile fluid made in the liver is stored in the gall bladder.

• The gall bladder can hold up to 1.6 fl. oz. of bile.

• After a meal, bile pours from the liver along the main bile duct, and from the gall bladder along the cystic duct into the small intestine.

• Bile helps to digest the fats and oils in foods.

• The liver makes up to two pints of bile each day.

THE LIVER'S TASKS

The liver has more than 500 known tasks in the body, and probably more that haven't yet been discovered. Some of the main ones are:

• Breaking down nutrients and other substances from digestion brought direct to the liver from the small intestine.

• Storing vitamins for times when they may be lacking in food.

• Making bile, a digestive juice.

• If levels of blood sugar are too low, changing body starch back into blood sugar and releasing it.

• Breaking apart old, dead, worn-out red blood cells.

• Breaking down toxins and possibly harmful substances, like alcohol and poisons.

• Helping to control the amount of water in blood

and body tissues.

• If levels of blood sugar are too high, changing this into body starch and storing it.

Alcohol is a toxins thatthe liver breaks down and makes harmless. Too much alcohol can overload the liver and cause a serious disease called *cirrhosis*.

BOX HEADINGS
Look for heading words linked to your research to guide you to the right fact box.

JUST THE FACTS
Each topic box presents the facts you need in short, quick-to-read bullet points.

6–7 Body Systems

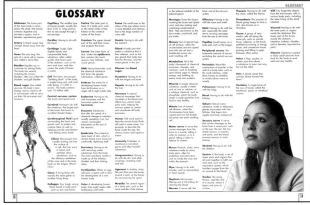

58–59 Glossary

EXTRA INFORMATION

The black box on the right hand side of the page explains a new aspect of the main topic.

LINKS

Look for the purple links throughout the book. Each link gives details of other pages where related or additional facts can be found.

- See pages 36–37 for information on the blood.

CUTAWAY DIAGRAMS

Clear, accurate diagrams show how the parts of the body fit together.

GLOSSARY

- A GLOSSARY of words and terms used in this book begins on page 58.
- The glossary words provide additional information to supplement the facts on the main pages.

HOW THE PANCREAS WORKS

Fatty foods, such as fries, are broken apart by enzymes made in the pancreas.

- Pancreas has two main jobs.
- One is to make hormones.
- The other is to make digestive chemicals called *pancreatic juices*.
- These juices contain about 15 powerful enzymes that break apart many substances in foods, including proteins, carbohydrates, and fats.
- Pancreas makes about 3 pints of digestive juices daily.
- During a meal, these pass along the pancreatic duct tubes into the small intestine to digest foods there.

- See page 52 for information on hormones.

WHEN THINGS GO WRONG

A yellowish tinge to the skin and eyes is known as *jaundice*. It is often a sign of liver trouble.

Usually, the liver breaks down old red blood cells and gets rid of the coloring substance in bile fluid. If something goes wrong, the coloring substance builds up in blood and skin and causes jaundice. *Hepatitis*, an infection of the liver, can cause jaundice.

UNUSUAL SUPPLY

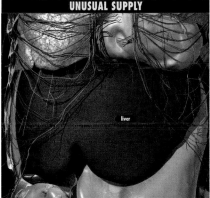

liver

One of the liver's main functions is to break down nutrients for the body. This means the liver has a unique blood supply.

- Most body parts are supplied with blood flowing along one or a few main arteries.
- The liver has a main artery, the *hepatic artery*.
- The liver also has a second and much greater blood supply.
- This comes along a vessel called the *hepatic portal vein*.

- The hepatic portal vein is the only main vein that does not take blood straight back to the heart.
- It runs from the intestines to the liver, bringing blood full of nutrients from digestion.

- See pages 36–37 for information on the BLOOD.

BABY LIVER

Most babies and young children have big abdomens. This is partly because their liver is much larger in proportion to the body's overall size, than the liver of an adult.

- An adult liver is usually $\frac{1}{40}$ of total body weight.
- A baby's liver is nearer $\frac{1}{20}$ of total body weight.

Babies and toddlers often have a tummy that sticks out, but it's not the stomach that causes this shape, it's their liver.

WHAT IS THE LIVER?

liver

The liver is the largest single organ inside the body.

- Wedge-shaped, dark red in color.
- Typical weight 3.3 lbs.
- Depth at widest part on right side 6 in.
- Has a larger right lobe and smaller left lobe.
- Lobes separated by a strong layer, the *falciform ligament*.

WHAT IS THE PANCREAS?

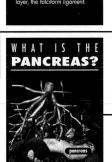

pancreas

The pancreas is a long, slim, wedge-shaped organ.

- It is soft, greyish-pink in color.
- Typical weight 3.5 oz.
- Typical length 6 in.
- Has three main parts: *head* (wide end), *body* (middle) and *tail* (tapering end).

43

PICTURE CAPTIONS

Captions explain what is in the pictures.

BODY SYSTEMS

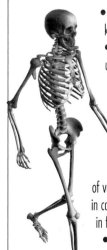

T he body is often divided into body systems. Each system, though performing specific jobs, works together with the other systems. Body systems are made from microscopic building blocks, called *cells*. A typical cell is only 0.011 inches across. There are about 10 trillion cells in the body.

There are many different kinds of cells, such as nerve cells and muscle cells. Many cells of the same kind form tissue, such as nerve and muscle tissue. Two or more different kinds of tissue create an organ, like the brain, stomach, or kidney. Several organs working together to carry out one major function, such as digesting food, are known as a *body system*.

INTEGUMENTARY SYSTEM

- The skin, hair, and nails.
- Protects internal organs from physical wear, dirt, water, sun's rays, and harm.
- Skin keeps in essential body fluids, salts and minerals.
- Helps to control body temperature by sweating and flushing to lose heat, or going pale with goosebumps to retain heat.
- Provides sense of touch (see Sensory System).
- Gets rid of small amounts of waste substances in sweat.

MUSCULAR SYSTEM

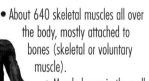

- About 640 skeletal muscles all over the body, mostly attached to bones (skeletal or voluntary muscle).
- Muscle layers in the walls of inner parts like the stomach and intestines (visceral or involuntary muscle).
- Muscle in the walls of the heart (heart muscle or myocardium).
- Muscles contract to produce all forms of bodily movement.
- Sometimes combined with bones and joints as the musculoskeletal system.

SKELETAL SYSTEM

- 208 bones and the various kinds of joints between them.
- Gives physical support to hold up the body's soft, floppy parts.
- Gives protection to certain body parts like the brain, eyes, heart, lungs.
- Pulled by muscles, to allow movement.
- Acts as a store or reservoir of valuable minerals like calcium, in case these are in short supply in food.
- Sometimes combined with muscles as the musculoskeletal system.

NERVOUS SYSTEM

- The brain, spinal cord, and peripheral nerves.
- Controls and coordinates all body processes, from breathing and heartbeat, to making movements.
- Allows mental processes, such as thoughts, recalling memories, and making decisions.
- Sensory nerves bring information from the sense organs and other sensors.
- Motor nerves carry instructions to muscles about movement and to glands about releasing their products.
- Works with the hormonal system.

SENSORY SYSTEM

- The eyes, ears, nose, tongue, and skin make up the five main sets of sensory organs.
- Sensors inside the body monitor for temperature, blood pressure, oxygen levels, positions of joints, amount of stretch in muscles, and many other changes.
- Gravity and motion sensors in the inner ear contribute to the process of balance.
- Sometimes included as part of the nervous system, since the main sense organs are in effect the specialized endings of sensory nerves.

RESPIRATORY SYSTEM

- Includes the nose, windpipe, main chest airways, and lungs.
- Obtains essential oxygen from the air around and passes it to the blood for distribution.
- Gets rid of waste carbon dioxide, which would be poisonous if it built up in the blood.
- Also provides the ability to make vocal sounds and speech.

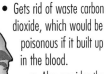

CIRCULATORY (CARDIOVASCULAR) SYSTEM

- The heart, blood vessels, and blood.
- The heart provides pumping power to send blood all around the body.
- Blood spreads vital oxygen, nutrients, hormones, and other substances to all body parts.
- Blood collects wastes and unwanted substances from all body parts.
- Blood clots seal wounds and cuts.
- Closely involved with the immune system for fighting disease.

DIGESTIVE SYSTEM

- Mouth, teeth, throat, esophagus, stomach, intestines, rectum, and anus make up the digestive passageway or tract.
- Liver, gall bladder, and pancreas are also part of the digestive system.
- Digests food into nutrients tiny enough to take into the body.
- Gets rid of leftovers as solid wastes.
- Nutrients provide energy for all life processes and raw materials for growth, maintenance, and repairing everyday use.

URINARY SYSTEM

- The kidneys, ureters, bladder, and urethra.
- Filters blood to get rid of unwanted substances and wastes.
- Forms unwanted substances and wastes into liquid waste or urine.
- Stores and releases urine.
- Controls amount and concentration of blood and body fluids, called *water balance*, by adjusting amount of water lost in urine.

REPRODUCTIVE SYSTEM

- The only system which differs significantly in females and males.
- The only system which is not working at birth, but starts to function at puberty.
- The male system produces sperm cells continually, millions per day.
- The female system produces egg cells, about one every 28 days, during the menstrual cycle.
- If an egg cell joins a sperm cell to form an embryo, the female system nourishes this as the egg grows into a baby inside the womb.

HORMONAL (ENDOCRINE) SYSTEM

- About ten main parts called *endocrine* or *hormone-making glands*.
- Some organs with other main tasks, like the stomach and heart, also make hormones.
- Hormones spread around the body in blood.
- Closely linked to the nervous system for coordinated control of inner-body processes.
- Closely linked with reproductive system..

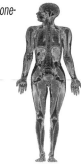

LYMPHATIC SYSTEM

- The lymph vessels, lymph nodes (glands), lymph ducts, and lymph fluid.
- Gathers general body fluids from between cells and tissues.
- One-way flow channels fluid through the lymph network of nodes and vessels.
- Helps to distribute nutrients and collect wastes.
- Lymph fluid empties into blood system.
- Closely linked with to immune system.

IMMUNE SYSTEM

- Defends the body against invading dangers such as bacteria, viruses and other microbes.
- Gets rid of debris in tissues from normal use.
- Helps the body recover from disease and illness.
- Helps repair injuries and normal use.
- Keeps watch for problems and disease processes arising inside the body, such as malignant (cancerous) cells.

THE SKIN

WHERE IN THE BODY?

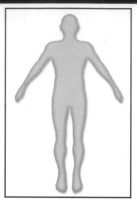

The skin is a tough but flexible layer that covers the entire body. It helps to control temperature and protects internal organs from damage.

When you look at yourself in the mirror, most of what you see—skin, hair and nails—is not living. Just underneath this dead surface, however, skin is very much alive, and very busy, too—as you know if you're unlucky enough to scratch or cut yourself. Skin is the body's largest single organ. It has at least ten main tasks, which include providing your sense of touch. It wears away every month—but it replaces itself every month, too.

SKIN MICROPARTS

An average patch of skin 0.15 sq. in. (the size of a fingernail) contains:

- 5 million microscopic cells of at least 12 main kinds.

- 100 tiny holes, called *pores,* for releasing sweat.

- 1,000 micro-sensors of about six main shapes for detecting various features of touch.

- more than 100 hairs.

- About 3.2 ft. of blood vessels.

- About 20 in. of micronerves.

- About 100 of the tiny glands that make sebum, a natural waxy-oily substance that keeps skin supple and fairly waterproof.

TOUCH

Your sense of touch or feeling is more complicated than it seems. It is not just a single sense, detecting physical contact. It is a multi-sense detecting:

- Light contact, such as a brush from a feather.

- Heavy pressure, such as being pushed or squeezed hard.

- Cold, like an ice-cube.

- Heat, such a hot water.

- Movement, including tiny, fast vibrations. Your fingertip skin can detect vibrations that are too small for your eyes to see.

- Surface texture, such as rough wood or smooth plastic.

- Moisture content, from dry sand to wet mud.

Wearing warm clothes in winter helps protect our skin from feeling the cold.

DANGEROUS SWEAT

A person can lose 10.5–15 pints of sweat before the body suffers from the loss of important salts and minerals.

EXTRA SENSITIVE

- Skin on the fingertips has more than 465 microsensors per square inch, to give the most sensitive touch.

- It has more sweat glands that make a thin layer of sweat on the skin that helps you to grip better.

- It also has tiny ridges or swirls to give even better grip. These form the pattern of your fingerprints.

- Every set of fingerprints for every person around the world is different—even between identical twins.

A thin layer of sweat on the fingertips helps you grip objects better.

SWEAT FACTS

Total number of sweat glands	**3–5 million**
Total length of tubes in all sweat glands stretched out straight and joined end-to-end	**31 miles**
Amount of sweat on average day	**10–17 fl. oz.**
Amount of sweat on a cold day	**2.3 fl. oz.**

LAYERS OF THE SKIN

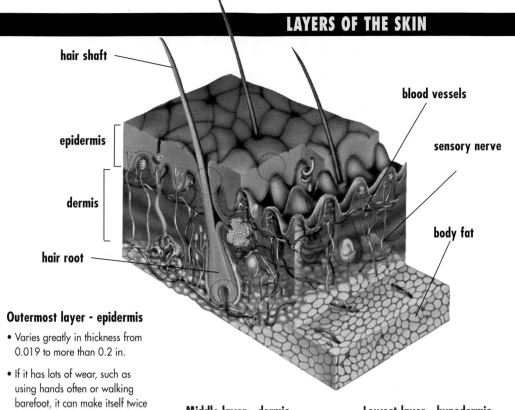

- hair shaft
- epidermis
- dermis
- hair root
- blood vessels
- sensory nerve
- body fat

Outermost layer - epidermis

- Varies greatly in thickness from 0.019 to more than 0.2 in.

- If it has lots of wear, such as using hands often or walking barefoot, it can make itself twice as thick as normal, for extra protection. This is called a *callus*.

Microscopic cells at its base multiply fast, fill with the tough substance keratin, move outward, become flatter and die, and form the surface layer which is continually rubbed away.

Middle layer - dermis

- Contains sweat glands, hair roots (follicles), most of the microsensors for touch, and tiny blood vessels called *capillaries*.

- Also contains fibers of the substances *collagen* for strength and *elastin* for elasticity.

Lowest layer - hypodermis

- Contains mainly body fat, which works as a cushion against knocks and pressure.

- Works as an insulator to keep in body warmth.

• See pages 36–37 for information on blood circulation.

MICROSENSORS

- The largest touch micro-sensors are called *Pacinian sensors*. They have many layers like tiny onions and are up to 0.019 in. across. They detect hard pressure.

- The smallest microsensors are 100 times smaller and feel light touch.

SHED SKIN

- Each minute about 50,000 tiny flakes of skin are rubbed off or fall from the body.

- This loss is natural and is made up by microscopic cells at the base of the epidermis multiplying rapidly.

- This happens so fast that the epidermis replaces itself about every month.

- Over a lifetime the body sheds more than 88 lbs. of skin.

SKIN THICKNESS

Skin makes itself thicker where it is worn or rubbed more. On average:

- Soles of feet - 0.2 in. or more
- Back 0.1–0.15 in.
- Palms of hands - 0.08–0.15 in.
- Scalp on head - 0.06 in.
- Fingertips - 0.04 in.
- Average body 0.04–0.08 in.
- Eyelids - 0.019 in.

• See pages 22–23 for information on eye.

0.2

0.1

MAIN TASKS OF THE SKIN

Protection

- Provides protection from knocks and bumps.

- Keeps out dirt, germs, and liquids. like water.

- Shields the body from the sun's dangerous rays (especially ultraviolet, UV), perhaps by going darker (suntan).

Keeps fluids in

- Keeping in valuable body fluids, minerals, and salts.

Touch

- Provides sense of touch.

Temperature control

- Cools the body if it gets too hot.

- Keeps heat inside the body in cold conditions.

Vitamin D

- Produces an important nutrient, vitamin D, that keeps you healthy.

Waste removal

- Removes of some waste products (through sweat).

Anti-germ layer

- Produces germ-killing substances to form a layer on skin.

SIZE OF THE SKIN

Area

A typical adult's skin, taken off and ironed flat, would cover some 6.5 sq. feet—about the area of a single bed or a small shower curtain.

Weight

The weight of the skin is about 6.6–8.8 lbs. for a typical adult—twice as heavy as the next-largest organ, the liver.

HAIR & NAILS

HAIR & NAILS

Hairs and nails, like the epidermis, the outer layer of skin, are dead. Your body has hairs all over, except for a few places, like your palms, the palm sides of your fingers, and the soles of your feet. However, some hairs grow thicker and longer, and so we notice them more. These are the hairs on the head, eyebrows, and eyelashes. As we grow up, hairs also appear under the arms, called *axillary hair*, and between the legs.

WHERE IN THE BODY?

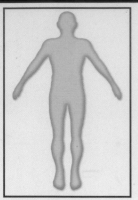

Hair is found almost all over our bodies. Nails grow at the end of each toe and finger.

WHY HAVE EYELASHES AND EYEBROWS?

Eyebrow hairs

Help to stop sweat dripping into the eyes.

Eyelash hairs

Help to whisk away bits of windblown dust, dirt, and pests like insects from th e eyes.

NAIL GROWTH

- Most nails grow about 0.019 in. each week.
- In general, fingernails grow faster than toenails.
- Nails grow faster in summer than in winter.
- If you're right-handed, nails on your right hand grow faster than those on your left, and the other way round if you're left-handed.

EYEBROWS AND EYELASHES

inches of hair growth per month

Bar chart showing hair growth per month, with vertical axis marked 0 in, 0.25 in, and 0.5 in. Bars: Scalp Hair (tallest, near 0.5 in), Eyebrow (about 0.2 in), Eyelash (about 0.2 in).

- Scalp hairs grow 0.011–0.015 in. each day, which is almost 0.5 in. each month.

- Eyebrow hairs grow slowly, only 0.0005 in. per day, reaching a greatest length of 0.2 in.

- Eyelash hairs grow at a similar rate to eyebrow hairs, but usually stop growing at 0.27–0.31 in. long.

• See pages 22–23 for information on eyes.

THE THICKNESS OF A HAIR

- Most scalp hairs are around 0.0019 in. thick, so 500 in a row would be almost 1 in. thick.

- Light colored hairs are usually thinner than dark hairs.

- Eyelashes are thicker, up to 0.003 in.

NAIL PARTS

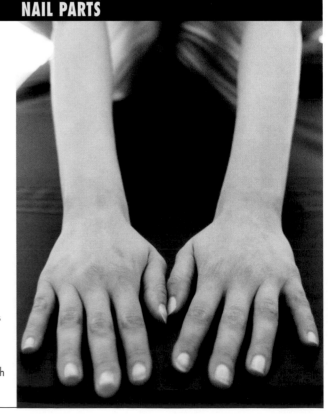

Finger nails have many different parts.

Nail plate
The main flat part of the nail.

Free edge
The end of the nail which you trim, not attached to the underlying finger or toe.

Nail bed
The underside of the nail plate, which is attached to the underlying flesh but slides slowly along as it grows.

Lunula
The pale 'half-moon' where the youngest part of the nail emerges from the flesh of the finger or toe.

Eponychium
The cuticle fold where the nail base disappears under the flesh of the finger or toe.

Nail root
The growing part of the nail, hidden in the flesh of the finger or toe.

HAIR STRUCTURE AND THICKNESS

- Hairs are glued-together rods of dead, flattened, microscopic cells filled with the tough, hard body substance, called *keratin*.

- A hair grows at its root, which is buried in a pocket-like pit in the skin, called the *follicle*.

- Extra cells are added to the root, which pushes the rest of the hair up out of the skin.

- The part of the hair above the root is called the *shaft*.

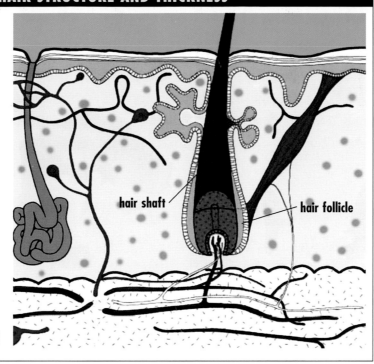

hair shaft

hair follicle

• See pages 8–9 for information on THE SKIN.

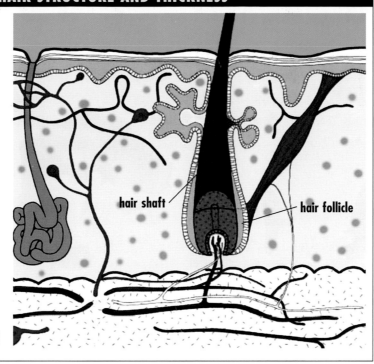

HAIR — WHY HAVE IT?

Protection
- Head hair protects against bangs and bruises.
- It also shields the top of the head, and the delicate brain inside, from heat or cold.

Warmth
- Body hairs stand on end when you're cold, each pulled by a tiny muscle attached to its root, called the *erector pili muscle*.
- These "goosebumps" around the body helps to trap air and keeps in body warmth.

Safety
- Our hair can also stand on end when we feel frightened. When our body hairs were longer, in prehistoric times, the 'hair-raising' also made us look bigger and more impressive to enemies.

HAIR GROWTH

Different kinds of hairs grow at different rates.

- Because most scalp hairs grow for only 3-5 years, their maximum length is 20–31 in. before they fall out and are replaced.

- However, some people have unusual hair that falls out much less often, and can reach lengths of 26 feet.

Hair growth in thin, fair hair is slower than in thick, dark hair.

NUMBER OF HAIRS

The number of hairs on the head varies according to the color of the hair. In a typical adult, the number is:

Fair hair	130,000
Brown	110,000
Black	100,000
Red	90,000

• See page 51 for SIGNS OF AGING

HAIR LIFE CYCLES

Most kinds of hairs grow for a time, gradually slow down in growth rate, then hardly grow at all.

- After this final slow down, they usually fall out and are replaced by new hairs growing up from the same follicles in the skin.

- This means, on average, about 100 hairs are lost from the head every day.

- In eyebrow hairs, the life cycle lasts about 20 weeks.

- In eyelash hairs, the life cycle lasts around 10 weeks.

- In scalp hairs, this life cycle lasts up to 5 years.

FASTER HAIR GROWING

- Hair growth is faster at night than during the day.

- Hair growth is faster in summer than in winter.

- Hair growth is faster around the ages of 15–25 years than any other time.

NAILS — WHY HAVE THEM?

A nail is a strong, stiff, dead, flat plate made of the same dead substance as hairs, keratin. Each nail acts as a flat, rigid pad on the back of the fingertip.

Touch
- When you press gently on an object, the fingertip is squeezed between it and the nail.
- This makes it easier to judge pressure and the hardness of the object. Without a nail, the whole fingertip would bend back.

Scratching
- You also use nails to scratch and get rid of objects on the skin.

MUSCLES AND MOVEMENT

Muscles power all of your body's movements, from blinking to jumping high in the air. Muscle actions are controlled by messages from your brain along nerves called *motor nerves*. Muscles are the body's largest single system and are found throughout the body. Half of a grown human being's body weight is from their muscles.

• See pages 20–21 for information on the brain.

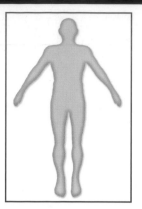

Muscles are found throughout the body. They help us to move, from walking to lifting objects.

SAVE ENERGY – GIVE A SMILE

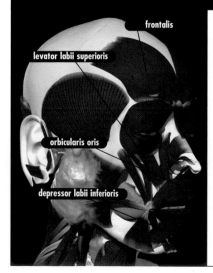

- All muscles need energy to work, which is brought by the blood in the form of blood sugar (glucose).
- You use about 40 facial muscles to frown, but only half as many to smile.

• See pages 36–37 for information on BLOOD.

TYPES OF MUSCLE

The body has three main kinds of muscles: skeletal, visceral, and cardiac.

- Skeletal muscles are mostly attached to the bones of the skeleton and pull on them to make you move.

- These are the ones we normally mean when we talk about muscles.

- Skeletal muscles are also called *voluntary muscles*, because you can control them at will just by thinking.

- Skeletal muscles are also called *striped* or *striated muscles* because under the microscope they have a pattern of stripes or bands.

- Visceral muscles form sheets, layers, or tubes in the walls of the inner body parts (viscera) like the stomach and bladder.

- Visceral muscles are also called *involuntary muscles* because they work automatically.

- Visceral muscles are also called *smooth muscles* because under the microscope they lack any pattern of stripes or bands.

- The third type of muscle is *cardiac muscle*, which forms the walls of the heart.

• See pages 32–33 for information on THE HEART.

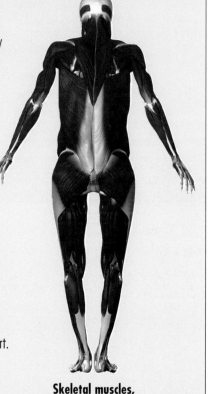

Skeletal muscles, seen from the back.

MUSCLES THAT MAKE FACES

We use our muscles to communicate and send information—and not just by speaking, which uses about 40 muscles. We also use muscles for facial expressions.

Muscle name	Site	What it does	Expression
Frontalis	Forehead	Raises eyebrows	Surprise
Procerus	Between eyes	Pulls eyebrows in and down	Stern, concentration
Auricularis	Above and to side of ear	Wiggles ear (only for some people)	
Buccinator	Cheek	Moves cheek	Blowing, sucking
Risorius	Side of mouth	Pulls corner of mouth	Grin
Depressor labii	Under lip	Pulls lower lip down	Frown

frontalis

levator labii superioris

orbicularis oris

depressor labii inferioris

Face muscles allow us to make a huge range of expressions.

INSIDE A MUSCLE

A muscle is a bundle of fibers. These bundles are called *fascicles*. Within each fiber is a group of fibrils. A single fibril contains myosin and actin filaments. These slide past each other to shorten the muscle.

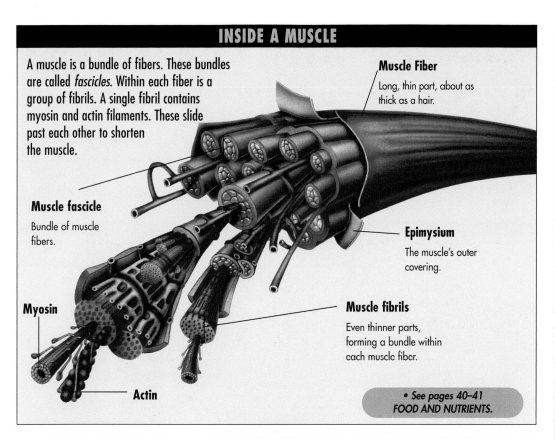

Muscle Fiber
Long, thin part, about as thick as a hair.

Muscle fascicle
Bundle of muscle fibers.

Epimysium
The muscle's outer covering.

Myosin

Muscle fibrils
Even thinner parts, forming a bundle within each muscle fiber.

Actin

• See pages 40–41
FOOD AND NUTRIENTS.

• See pages 40–41 FOOD AND NUTRIENTS.

MUSCLE POWER COMPARED

This list shows the power of the body's muscle compared to various machines, in watts (the scientific units of power).

Laser-pen pointer	0.002
Heart by itself	2
All the body's muscles working hard	100
Family car on the highway	100,000
Space shuttle	10,000 million

INDIVIDUAL VARIATIONS

• Some people have very small versions of certain muscles or none at all. This is part of the natural variation between different people.

• For example, a few people lack the thin, sheet-like muscle in the neck, called the *platysma*.

HOW MUSCLES WORK

Muscles work by contracting and pulling their ends closer together.

• In most skeletal muscles, the ends taper to rope-like tendons, which are joined firmly to bones.

• Muscles cannot push or forcefully get longer, they are stretched longer when other muscles work elsewhere.

• Muscles contain two body substances, or *proteins*, called *actin* and *myosin*, which are shaped like long threads.

• In each muscle, millions of these threads slide past each other to make the whole muscle shorten.

• Most muscles can shorten or contract to about two-thirds their resting length.

• A muscle bulges in the middle when it shortens but its overall size or volume does not change.

Exercise can increase the size of muscles, but they have no effect on the actual number of muscles or the number of muscle cells— this stays the same.

MUSCLE RECORDS

• There are about 640 main skeletal muscles.

• They form about two-fifths of the body weight in adult men, and slightly less, about one-third of body weight, in adult women, girls, and boys.

• Plenty of exercise and activity makes muscles grow bigger and stronger. They can form up to half of body weight.

MUSCLE RECORDS

Bulkiest
The gluteus maximus, forming most of the buttock. It works when you pull your thigh back to push your body forward when you walk, run, and jump.

Smallest
The stapedius, deep in the ear. When the ear detects very loud noises it pulls on the body's smallest bone, the stirrup (stapes), to prevent it moving too much and damaging the delicate inner parts of the ear.

Longest
The sartorius, which runs from the side of the hip down across the front of the thigh to the inner side of the knee.

Most powerful for its size
The masseter, which runs from the cheekbone to the lower side of the lower jaw and bulges when you chew.

Busiest
The orbicularis oculi, better known as the eyelid muscles. They work up to 50,000 times each day as you blink and wink.

Biggest tendon
The calcaneal tendon, which joins the calf muscles to the heel bone. It takes the strain when you stand on tip-toe and is often called the *Achilles tendon*.

THE SKELETON

Your skeleton consists of all the bones in your body—over 200 of them. It's like an inner framework that supports the softer body parts such as organs, nerves, and blood vessels. Your skeleton is not fixed and stiff. It is a moving framework that muscles pull into hundreds of different positions every day.

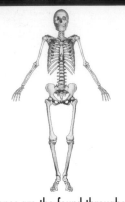

Bones are the found throughout the body. Flexible parts of the body, such as fingers and toes, have more bones.

BONES NOT JOINED TO OTHER BONES

There are three bones in the body not joined to any other bone.

Hyoid

A U-shaped bone in the front of the upper neck, near the throat and the base of the tongue.

Kneecap or patella

This is inside a muscle tendon and slides over the front of the knee joint, helping to protect it.

SIZE AND VARIATIONS

Our bones are a strong inner framework that hold up the soft inner parts of the body.

- There is no truth in the old belief that men and women have different numbers of ribs. Both have 24 ribs, as 12 pairs.

- However, the total number of bones varies slightly as part of natural differences between people.

- For example, about one person in 20 (man or woman) has an extra pair of ribs, making 21 pairs instead of the usual 20.

- There are more bones, over 300, in the skeleton of a baby.

- As the baby grows, some of these enlarge and fuse together to make bigger single bones.

- The skeleton forms about one-seventh of the body's total weight.

• See pages 50–51 for information on STAGES OF LIFE.

TAIL END

The lowest part of the backbone is called the *coccyx*. It's made of three to five smaller bones fused together into one, shaped like a small prong. It is all that is left of the long tail that our very distant ancestors had, millions of years ago, when they looked like monkeys and lived in trees.

Monkeys and humans are descended from the same distant ancestors.

WHAT ARE BONES LIKE?

Imagining our bodies as various everyday objects can help us to understand how they work.

Levers

The long bones of the arms and legs work like levers, with their pivot, or fulcrum, at the joint.

A bicycle chain

The many separate bones or vertebrae of the backbone only move slightly compared to each other. But over the whole backbone, this movement adds up to allow bending double, like the links of a bicycle chain.

A cage

The ribs work like the moveable bars of a cage. This protects the heart and lungs, yet gets bigger and smaller as the lungs breathe in and out.

An eggshell

The dome shape of the cranium around the brain is a very strong design, like an eggshell. Any sharp ridges or corners would weaken it.

• See pages 16–17 for information on BONES AND JOINTS.

NOT ALL BONE

Most of a baby's skeleton is made of cartilage, not bone.

- Most bones of the skeleton begin not as real bone, but as a slightly softer, bendier, smooth substance called *cartilage* (gristle).

- In a developing baby, the shapes of the eventual bones form first as cartilage.

- Then, as the baby grows into a child, the cartilage shapes become hardened into real bones.

- Even in the adult skeleton, some bones are partly cartilage.

- For example, the front end of each rib, where it joins to the breastbone, is made not of bone but of cartilage called *costal cartilage*.

- The nose and ears are mainly cartilage, not bone, which is why they are slightly flexible.

SKELETON STRENGTH

Our skeleton is made of living bones that can mend themselves if broken.

- The bones of the skeleton are stronger, size for weight, than almost every kind of wood or plastic.

- If the skeleton was made of steel, it would weigh four times as much.

- The thigh bone can stand a pressure of 21 tons per sq. in. when we jump and land.

- The skeleton can also mend itself, which no kind of plastic or metal can.

NUMBERS OF BONES

A human skeleton contains, on average, 206 bones. They are divided in different groups through the body:

Skull

Cranium (brain case) 8

Face 14

Ear 3 tiny bones each

Total: 28 bones

Throat (hyoid bone) 1

Backbone

Neck (cervical vertebrae) 7

Chest (thoracic vertebrae) 12

Lower back (lumbar vertebrae) 5

Base of back (sacrum, coccyx) 2

Total: 26 bones

Rib cage

Ribs 24

Breastbone 1

Total: 25 bones

Arms

Shoulder 2

Upper arm 1

Forearm 2

Wrist 8

Palm 5

Fingers and thumb 14

Total: 32 bones in each arm (includes hand)

Legs

Hip 1

Thigh and knee 2

Shin 2

Ankle 7

Sole of foot 5

Toes 14

Total: 31 bones in each leg (includes foot)

SKELETON'S MAIN TASKS

The main tasks of the skeleton are to:

- Hold up the body, giving support to softer parts.
- Allow the body to move when pulled by muscles.
- Provide openings for the nose and mouth to breathe and eat.
- Protect certain body parts, for example, the upper skull around the brain, the front skull around most of the eyes, and the ribs around the lungs and chest.
- Store many body minerals, such as calcium and magnesium, for times when food is scarce and these minerals are in short supply for other body processes, like sending nerve messages.
- Make new microscopic cells for the blood, at the rate of 3 million every second. These cells are produced in the soft jelly-like bone marrow found in the centers of some bones.

The skeleton provides some protection for vital body parts, but it is helpful to provide extra protection, such as a helmet when riding a bike.

Your skeleton holds you up, but you would not be able to move if it was not for the joints that link your bones together. More than half of your body's bones—112 out of 206—are in your wrists, hands, fingers, ankles, feet, and toes. So are more than half of your 200-plus joints. Your bones, muscles and joints work so closely together that they are sometimes viewed as a single system, called the *musculoskeletal system.*

WHERE IN THE BODY?

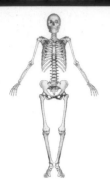

Joints allow the skeleton to move. They can be found all over the body.

PARTS OF A BONE

Periosteum

The outer covering wrapped all around the bone.

Foramen

Small hole in a bone, where a nerve or blood vessel passes inside.

Compact bone

Very strong, hard outer layer of bone, like a shell.

Osteons (Haversian systems)

Tiny cells of bone substance bundled and glued together to make compact bone.

Spongy or cancellous bone

Inner layer of a bone, under the compact bone, that has holes like a sponge.

Marrow

Jelly-like substance in the center of most bones.

Red marrow

Found in all bones of a baby, but only in the long bones of the arms and legs, ribs, backbone, breastbone and upper skull in an adult. Makes new microscopic cells for the blood.

Yellow marrow

In adults, found mainly in smaller bones of the hands and feet. Contains fat for use as an energy reserve, but can change to red marrow if needed.

BONE MAKE UP

- The word *skeleton* comes from an ancient word meaning *dried up*. But living bones are not dry, they are about one-quarter water. (Overall, the body is two-thirds water.)

- The main minerals in bone are calcium, phosphate, and carbonate. These form tiny crystals which give bone its hardness and stiffness.

- Bone also contains tiny fibers of the substance collagen, which makes it slightly flexible under pressure, and less likely to snap.

- If a bone is soaked in a special acid chemical, the crystals of calcium phosphate and calcium carbonate are removed. Only the collagen fiber are left. This means that it is so flexible that a long bone like the upper-arm bone can be tied in a knot.

During long space flights, the lack of gravity puts bones under less preasure than they are on Earth. The bones start to lose minerals and become weaker. Astronauts exercise regularly to keep their bones strong.

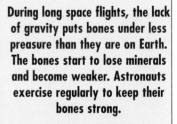

• See pages 40–41
FOOD AND NUTRIENTS

LIGAMENTS

Ligament   Muscle

Bones are held together at a joint by stretchy straps called *ligaments*, which stop them moving too far or coming apart.
If the bones slip and come out of their usual position, a dislocation occurs.

YES AND NO

The two topmost backbones (*cervical vertebrae*), just under the skull, have special joint designs. They allow the head to make important movements.

- The axis (uppermost) backbone has a curved shape like a saddle. It allows the head to tilt to the side and nod.

- The atlas (second uppermost) backbone is more like a ring and allows the head to turn or rotate to look to the side.

Nodding and shaking your head is only possible with two special joint designs in the backbone.

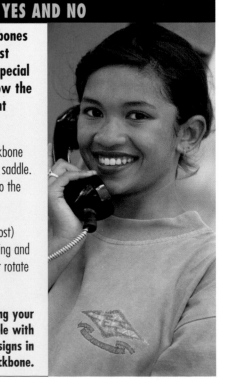

PARTS OF A BONE

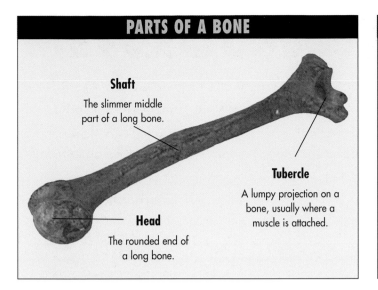

Shaft
The slimmer middle part of a long bone.

Tubercle
A lumpy projection on a bone, usually where a muscle is attached.

Head
The rounded end of a long bone.

BONE RECORDS

Longest
The thigh bone (femur), forming about one-quarter of total body height.

Widest
The hip bone (pelvis), forming the body's broadest part.

Smallest
The stirrup (stapes) deep inside the ear, a U shape just .031 in. long.

Toughest
The lower jaw (mandible), used hundreds of times daily when chewing.

DESIGN OF THE JOINT

The different designs of your body's joints are sometimes compared to machines and mechanical gadgets.

Hinge joint
Allows the bones to move only back and forth, not side to side (as in a door hinge).

Examples: knee and smaller knuckles of fingers.

Ball-and-socket joint
Allows the bones to move back and forth, side to side, and sometimes rotate.

Examples: hips, shoulders, largest knuckles.

Saddle joints
Shaped like a saddle for tilting and sliding.

Example: thumb.

Washer joints
Limited tilting with a pad or washer of cartilage between the bone ends.

Examples: joints between the backbones, where the cartilage pad is called the *intervertebral disc*.

Fixed or suture joint
No movement at all, because the bones are firmly joined together.

Examples: between the bones of the cranium (upper skull) around the brain.

REDUCING WEAR AND TEAR

- Where the ends of a bone touch in a joint, they are covered with smooth, glossy cartilage, to reduce wear and rubbing.

- The space between the bones is filled with a slippery liquid called *synovial fluid*, that reduces wear even more.

- The fluid is kept in by a loose bag around the joint, the *joint capsule*.

- New synovial fluid is always being made by the inner lining of this bag, called the *synovial membrane*.

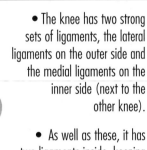

Even a large joint like the hip contains only about a teaspoon of synovial fluid.

BIGGEST JOINT

Your single biggest joint, the knee, has an unusual design with extra cartilages and ligaments.

- In addition to the cartilage covering the ends of the thigh and shin bones, the cartilage covers the knee with two pieces of moon-shaped cartilage.

- The cartilage pieces are called *menisci* and help the knee to lock straight so you can stand up easily.

- When atheletes have torn knee cartilage, it's usually one of these menisci which is damaged.

• See pages 12–13 for information on muscles.

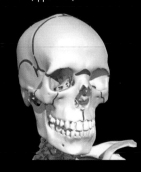

- The knee has two strong sets of ligaments, the lateral ligaments on the outer side and the medial ligaments on the inner side (next to the other knee).

- As well as these, it has two ligaments inside, keeping the ends of the bones very close together.

- These two ligaments form an X-like shape and are called *cruciate ligaments*.

Exercising and playing sports can sometimes damage your knee. It is important to always warm up.

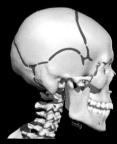

There are eight bones in the cranium. They are fused together to protect the brain underneath.

THE NERVOUS SYSTEM

The nervous system controls every movement and action we make, as well as every process that happens inside the body. Your nervous system is made up of your brain, spinal cord, and nerves. It works by sending tiny electrical signals, called *nerve impulses*. Millions of these travel around the body and brain every second.

Nerves run throughout the body, carrying electrical signals from the brain.

MAIN PARTS OF THE NERVOUS SYSTEM

There are two main nervous systems within the body. The central nervous system is the brain's main control center. It sends nerve impulses to the rest of the body using the peripheral nervous system. We have conscious control over the central and peripheral nervous systems.

Central nervous system:
Brain
Inside the top half of the head.
Spinal cord
The main nerve link between the brain and the body.

Peripheral nervous system:
Cranial nerves
Connect directly to the brain rather than the spinal cord. They go mainly to parts in the head like the eyes, ears, and nose.
Spinal nerves
Branch out from the spinal cord to the arms, legs, back, chest, and all other body parts.

• See pages 20–21 for information on THE BRAIN.

SLOW TO HURT

When you hurt a finger, you probably feel the touch first, and then the pain starts a moment later. This is because the signals about touch travel faster along the nerves than the signals about pain.

AUTOMATIC SYSTEM

- Some parts of the nerve system work automatically.

- Those processes are called the *autonomic nerve system*.

- They control heartbeat, food digestion, body temperature, and blood pressure.

We have no conscious control over some parts of our body, such as the systems that control digestion.

NERVES AND NERVE CELLS

A nerve's outer covering is called the *epineurium*. Inside are bundles of nerve fibers, called *axons*, each too small to see without a microscope.

epineurium

axons

• See pages 8–9 for information on THE SKIN.

NERVE SIGNALS

A nerve signal is a tiny pulse of electricity made by moving chemical substances into and out of the nerve cell.

- Average signal strength is $\frac{1}{10}$th of a volt.
- Average signal length is $\frac{1}{1000}$th of a second.
- Average recovery time before another signal can pass is $\frac{1}{500}$th of a second.
- Slowest signals travel 19 inches per second.
- Fastest signals travel 459 feet per second.

THICKEST NERVE

The sciatic nerve, in the hip and upper thigh, is about the width of its owner's thumb. This is thicker than the spinal cord, which is usually the width of its owner's little finger.

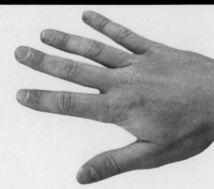

NERVES AND NERVE CELLS

Nerves are flexible but tough, so they can move easily at joints but withstand being squeezed by the muscles around them.

- Each nerve fiber is the long, wire-like part of a single microscopic nerve cell, called a *neuron*.

- Usually near one end, the nerve cell has a wider part, called the *cell body*.

- Branching from the nerve cell body are even thinner spidery-looking parts, called *dendrites*.

- Nerve messages from other nerve cells are picked up by the dendrites, processed and altered as they pass around the cell body, and then sent by the axon (fiber) to other nerve cells.

- Most nerve fibers are 0.0003 in. wide, so 4000 side by side would be just over 1 inch.

- They have a covering wrapped around them, called the *myelin sheath*. It makes nerve messages travel faster and stops them leaking away.

A typical nerve looks like wire or string.

SPINAL CORD

The spinal cord, in the back, is one of the most important parts of our nervous system.

- Joins the brain to the main body.

- Is about 17 in. long in a typical adult.

- Has 31 pairs of nerves branching left and right from it.

- Is protected inside a "tunnel" formed by a row of holes through the backbones.

- Like the brain, it has a layer of liquid around it, called *cerebrospinal fluid*, to cushion it from injury.

NERVE JUNCTIONS

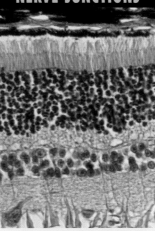

Synapses are so small that scientists have to use special electron microscopes to study them.

Each nerve cell receives signals from thousands of other cells and passes on signals to thousands more.

- Individual nerve cells do not actually touch each other where the ends of their dendrites and axons come together.

- The ends are separated by tiny gaps, at junction points, called *synapses*.

- The gap inside a synapse is just 1 microinch wide, which means 1 million in a row would stretch 1 inch.

- Nerve messages jump across a synapse not as electrical signals, but in the form of chemicals, called *neurotransmitters*.

- This chemical "jump" takes less than $\frac{1}{1,000}$th of a second.

NERVE LENGTHS

- All the nerves in the body, taken out and joined end to end, would stretch about 62 miles.

- The longest single nerve fibers, found in the legs, are up to 3 feet in length.

DIRECT TO THE BRAIN

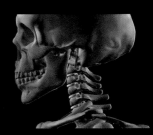

12 pairs of cranial nerves join directly to the brain and link it to the following parts:

1. Nose
For smelling

2. Eyes
For seeing

3. Eyeball-moving muscles

4. Eyeball-moving muscles

5. Skin and touch
On forehead, face, cheeks, jaw muscles, muscles for chewing

6. Eyeball-moving muscles

7. Tongue
For taste, saliva glands, tear glands, facial expressions

8. Ear
For hearing and balance

9. Rear of tongue
For taste, swallowing muscles

10. Swallowing muscles
Also lungs and heart in chest

11. Voicebox muscles
For speaking

12. Tongue muscles
For speaking and swallowing

NERVES TO EVERY PART

Nerves are connected to every body part.

- The thickest ones near the brain and spinal cord are known as *nerve trunks*.

- The thinnest ones spreading into body parts are called *terminal fibers*.

THE BRAIN

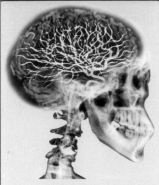

The brain is inside the cranium, forming the upper half of the head.

The brain contains more than 100 billion nerve cells, called *neurons*—about as many stars as in our galaxy, the Milky Way. The brain also contains perhaps ten times as many support cells, called *neuroglia*. It's not the size of a brain which makes it smart, or the number of cells. It depends on how often its owner uses it, and in how much detail—by looking, listening, learning, remembering, using imagination, and having ideas.

HUNGRY FOR ENERGY

- The brain consumes about one-fifth of all the energy used by the body.

- But the brain forms only about $\frac{1}{50}$th of the whole body.

- That means the brain uses ten times more energy for its size, compared to most other body parts.

- This energy is mainly in the form of blood sugar, called *glucose*, brought to the brain by its main blood vessels, the carotid and vertebral arteries.

- Average blood flow to the brain is 1.5 pints per minute, about one-eighth of the heart's total output.

- This flow is the same whether the body is at rest or very active.

- This is unusual because blood flow to other body parts changes greatly between rest and activity. For example, it increases to the muscle by ten times and decreases to the stomach by half.

- *See pages 34–35 for information on the CIRCULATORY SYSTEM*

CORTEX IN CONTROL

planning movement

making movement

speech

touch on the skin

hearing

vision

- The outer gray layer of the cerebrum, over the top of the brain, is called the *cerebral cortex*.

- Spread out flat, it would be the area of a pillowcase, and almost as thin.

- However, deep grooves, called *sulci*, are wrinkled and folded into the space inside the upper skull.

- The cortex has about half the brain's total number of nerve cells, around 50 billion.

- Each of these can have connections with more than 200,000 other nerve cells.

- The connections are made by the spidery-looking arms, called *dendrites*, and a much longer, wire-like part, the nerve fiber.

- The cortex is the main place where we become aware of what we see, hear, smell, taste, and touch..

- It is also the place where we plan movements and actions and get them started, known as *motor skills*.

- Each of these sensory and motor processes takes place in a different area of the cortex, known as a *center*.

- The cortex is also the major site for thinking and consciousness, what we call our "mind".

- The cortex is also involved in learning and memory, although scientists are not quite sure how.

- *See pages 22–27 for information on the senses.*

- *See pages 12–13 for information on muscles.*

THE WEIGHT OF THE BRAIN

The weight of an average adult brain is 3 pounds.

The largest accurately measured normal human brain is 6.3 pounds.

SIZE ISN'T EVERYTHING

- Bigger brains are not necessarily smarter, and there is no link between the size of a healthy brain and intelligence.

- The average female brain is slightly smaller than the average male brain.

- But the average female body is smaller, in comparison, to the average male body.

- Compared to body size, women have slightly larger brains than men.

MAIN BRAIN PARTS

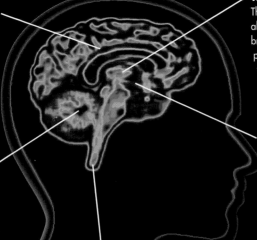

Cerebrum
The big wrinkled, domed part covering most of the top of the brain, forms more than four-fifths of the whole brain. It has a thin outer layer of "gray matter," the cerebral cortex, which is mainly nerve cells, covering an inner mass of "white matter," which is mainly nerve fibers.

Cerebellum
A smaller wrinkled part at the lower back, looks like a smaller version of the whole brain. in fact its name means *little brain*. It carries out detailed control of muscles so we can move about, keep our balance, and carry out skilled actions.

Thalamus
This is two egg-shaped parts almost at the center of the brain. It helps to sort and process information from four of the senses (sight, hearing, taste, and touch) going to the cerebrum above.

Hypothalamus
Just below and in front of the thalamus, is a main center for powerful feelings, emotions, and urges such as anger, fright, love, and joy.

The brain stem
At the base of the brain contains the main life support areas for heartbeat, breathing, blood pressure, and control of digestion. Its lower end merges into the top of the spinal cord.

HOLLOW BRAIN

- The brain has four small chambers inside it called *ventricles*.

- These arc filled with a pale liquid called *cerebrospinal fluid*, CSF.

- CSF is found around the brain, between two of the protective layers, called *meninges*, that surround it. CSF is also found in and around the spinal cord.

- The total amount of CSF inside and around the brain and spinal cord is about 4.2 fl.oz.

- This fluid flows very slowly and is gradually renewed about three times every 24 hours.

- CSF is important as it helps to cushion the brain from damage.

- The liquid also supports the brain within the skull, brings nourishment, and takes away wastes.

SLEEP

Even when asleep, the brain is just as active sending nerve messages around itself as it is when awake. This is shown by recordings of its electrical nerve signals.

- Older people tend to sleep more hours overall but often in several shorter sessions, such as "cat-naps" through the day.

- Usual sleep needs for most people every 24 hours:

New born	*20 hours*
10-year-old	*10 hours*
Adult	*7–8 hours*

LEFT AND RIGHT

- Nerve messages from the body cross over from left to right at the base of the brain.

- This means the left side of the brain receives signals from, and sends them to, the right side of the body.

- In most people, the left side of the brain is more active in speaking and reading, scientific skills, using numbers and maths, and working out problems in a logical way.

- The right side of the brain is more

active in dealing with shapes and colors, artistic skills like painting and music, and having creative ideas.

- In a right-handed person, the left side of the brain is generally dominant. In a left-handed person, the right side of the brain is generally dominant.

In a left-handed person, the right side of the brain is generally dominant.

THE GROWING BRAIN

The development of the brain happens quickly after conception. It continues to grow in size after birth and makes new nerve connections throughout childhood.

Inside the womb
- The brain is one of the first main body parts to form just three weeks after conception as a large arched bulge at the head end.

Four weeks after conception
- The brain is almost larger than the rest of the body.

20 weeks after conception
- Brain weighs about 3.5 oz.

At birth
- The brain is 14–17 oz., about one-third of its final adult size. In comparison, a new baby's body is about 1/25th of its final adult size.

Growing up
- By 3 years, the brain is approaching fully grown at 2.4 lbs.

- The brain does not make any new nerve cells after birth.

- The brain does make new connections between nerve cells, perhaps millions every week, as we take in knowledge, develop skills and learn new things.

From 20 years old onward
- The brain shrinks by about 0.03 oz. of weight per year. This represents the loss of around 10,000 nerve cells each day.

- Certain drugs, including alcohol, can speed this cell loss and make the brain shrink faster.

- See pages 50–51 for information on the STAGES OF LIFE.

EYES AND SIGHT

Each eyeball is in a bony bowl called the *eye socket*. It is formed by curved parts of five skull bones.

Experts believe that over half of the information we process comes in through our eyes, as words (through reading), pictures, drawings, real-life scenes, and images on screens. Yet the eye does not really see. It turns patterns of light rays into patterns of nerve signals, which go to the brain. The visual center at the back of the brain is the "mind's eye," where we recognize and understand what we see.

BLIND SPOT

The place where all the retina's nerve fibers come together to form the start of the optic nerve is called the *optic disc*.

- Since light cannot be detected here, it is known as the blind spot.
- Normally, we don't notice the blind spot because our eyes continually dart and look around at different parts of a scene.
- As we do this the brain guesses and "fills in" the missing area from what is around and what it has seen just before or after.
- The optic nerve contains one million nerve fibers—the most of any nerve carrying sense information to the brain.

FLOATERS

- Some people see spots or "floaters" that seem to be in front of the eye.
- These are actually in the vitreous humor jelly filling the inside of the eyeball.
- They are usually stray red blood cells or bits of fibers that have escaped from the retina.
- We can't look straight at them because as we move the eyeball, they move also.
- A few floaters are normal, but medical help is needed if they suddenly increase in number.

WHAT AN INCREDIBLE SIGHT

As it goes dark in the evening, what we see seems to lose color. This is because the cone cells work less, and we rely on the rods.

- The eye's inner lining, the retina, is where light rays are changed to nerve signals.
- The retina has an area about the same as a larger postage stamp.
- It has millions of microscopic cells that make nerve signals when hit by light rays.
- 125 million are rod cells, which work well in dim light, but cannot see colors, only shades of gray.

- 7 million are cone cells, which see fine details and colors, but work only in bright light.
- Most of the cones are concentrated in a slightly bowl-shaped hollow at the back of the retina, the *fovea*, or *yellow spot*.
- This is where light falls to give us the clearest, most detailed view.

> • See pages 18–19 for information on the nerves.

COLOR CONES

Many people who are red-green color blind can learn to tell colors apart by their shade or hue rather than the actual color.

- There are three kinds of light-detecting cone cells in the retina.
- They are called *red, green*, and *blue cones*.
- This is not because of their colors; they all look the same.
- The three types of cones detect three different colors of light.
- The brain works out the color of an object from the active cones.

- In some people, not all these cones are present or work properly.
- This is called *color blindness*, or *color vision deficiency*.
- Most common is when red and green are not seen very differently.
- This often runs in families and affects more males than females.
- True color blindness, seeing everything in shades of gray (like a black-and-white movie), is very rare, affecting less than 1 in 10,000 people.

MAIN PARTS OF THE EYE

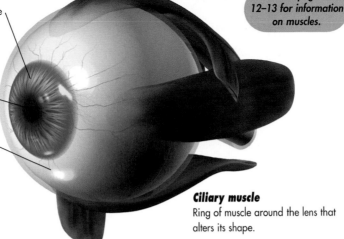

• See pages 12–13 for information on muscles.

Iris
Colored ring of muscle that can alter the size of the hole within it, the pupil, making it smaller in bright light to protect the delicate inside of the eye.

Pupil
Hole in the iris, through which light enters the eye's interior.

Sclera
Tough outer layer around the whole eye apart from the cornea.

Cornea
Thick clear dome at the front of the eye.

Conjunctiva
Sensitive covering at the front of the eyeball, over the cornea.

Lens
Pea-shaped blob about 0.4 in. across that alters in shape to see and focus clearly, from looking at faraway objects to nearby ones.

Retina
Inner layer lining the eyeball's interior.

Choroid
Blood-rich layer between sclera and retina.

Ciliary muscle
Ring of muscle around the lens that alters its shape.

Aqueous humor
Thin, clear fluid filling the space between the cornea and the lens.

Vitreous humor
Thick, clear jelly-like substance filling the main eyeball and giving its rounded shape.

MOVING THE EYEBALL

Behind the eyeball are six small ribbon-shaped muscles that make it turn and swivel in its socket or eye orbit.

Medial rectus
Moves the eye inward, toward the nose.

Lateral rectus
Moves the eye outward, away from the nose.

Superior rectus
Moves the eye upward, to look at the sky.

Inferior rectus
Moves the eye downward, to look at the floor.

Superior oblique
Pulls eye inwards and downwards.

Inferior oblique
Pulls eye upwards and outwards.

In total the eye can tilt as follows:

• look up by 35 degrees.
• look down by 50 degrees.
• look inward towards the nose by 50 degrees.
• look outward by 45 degrees.

IRIS SECURITY SCANS

Usually, people with darker skin and hair have browner irises. People with lighter skin and hair have bluer irises.

• Each person has a different color and detailed pattern of marks on the iris.
• Scans of the iris, fed into a computer, can be used like fingerprints for identification and security checks.
• Rarely does a person have two different colored irises, though it could happen at birth, or through injury.

• Every person in the world has different fingerprints, which can be used for identification and security checks.
• The same applies to the coloured part of the eye, the iris.

BLINKING AMAZING

• We spend about up to 30 minutes of our waking day with our eyes shut during blinks.
• Blinking washes soothing, cleansing tear fluid over the eye. The fluid washes away dust and helps to kill germs.
• Tear fluid comes from the lacrimal gland, just above and to the outer side of each eye, under a fold of skin.
• On average:
Number of blinks per minute: **6**
Length of blink: **0.3-0.4 seconds**
Total amount of tear fluid made in a day: **50 ml**
This can treble if surroundings are dusty or have chemical fumes.

MEASURING THE EYE

The eyeball is almost a perfect sphere or ball shape.

Side-to-side: 0.94 in.

Front-to-back: 0.94 in.

Top-to-bottom: 0.91 in.

• The eyeball's total weight is 0.8–1 oz.
• The eye is one of the body parts that grows least from birth to adulthood.

20/20 VISION

The saying *20/20 vision* came about from the way of describing how clearly a person can see.

• 20/20 means a person can see, at a distance of 20 feet, what normal eyesight can show.
• The larger the second number, the worse the eyesight.

• Someone with 20/60 vision can see at 20 feet what normal eyesight sees clearly at 60 feet.
• Nearsightedness, or *myopia*, is due to the eyeball being too long form front to back.

• Farsightedness, or *hypermetropia*, is due to the eyeball being too short from front to back.
• *Astigmatism* is when the curve of the eyeball is not the same in all directions.

EARS AND HEARING

W e can usually hear some kind of sound, whether it be the roar of a jet plane, friends talking, birds singing, or the wind rustling grass. Most of the time, we are not aware of sounds around us, because they tell us nothing new. The brain blocks out frequent noise like humming machinery or distant traffic. Only when we hear something new, important, or exciting, does the mind turn its attention to hearing.

The outer ear is on the side of the head, usually level with the nose. The inner ear is deep in the temporal skull bone, almost behind the eye.

OUTSIDE TO INSIDE

The ear is divided into three main sections:

Outer ear
Ear flap (*pinna* or *auricle*) and ear canal

Middle ear
Eardrum, tiny ear bones, and middle ear chamber

Inner ear
Cochlea, semi-circular canals, and their chambers

EAR BONES

- The body's six smallest bones, three in each middle ear.

- They were named long ago from items more common at the time, to do with horseriding and ironsmiths.

- Hammer (*malleus*) is attached to the eardrum.

- Anvil (*incus*) is the middle of the three.

- Stirrup (*stapes*) is attached to the oval window of the cochlea.

> • See pages 14–17 for information on bones.

STEREO HEARING

- Sound travels about 0.2 mi. per second in air.

- A sound from one side reaches the ear on that side more than 1,000th of a second before it reaches the other ear.

- The sound is louder and clearer in the closer ear, too.

- The brain can detect these differences in time, volume, and clarity, and work out the direction a sound comes from.

- This is known as *stereophonic hearing*.

- Headphones and earphones copy these differences to give the impression of directional sounds.

- Even sounds in front and behind can be told apart, whether they come from below or above.

- A sound from the floor directly in front causes some echoes and brings these mixed in with it.

- A sound from directly above has fewer echoes and reach the ears after the main sound.

> • See pages 20–21 for information on THE BRAIN.

THE SENSE OF BALANCE

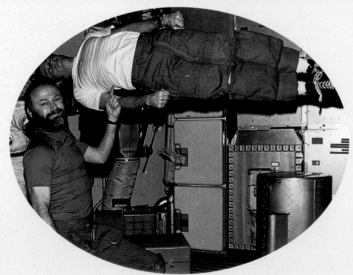

In space, there is no gravity to help give astronauts a sense of balance. The lack of gravity causes some people to develop motion sickness.

- Three semicircular canals in the ear are at right angles to each other.

- Each canal has a jelly-like blob at one end in its ampulla or widened part.

- There are microhairs in the jelly-like blob.

- As the head moves, fluid in the canal swishes and moves the jelly-like blob.

- This moves the hairs of the hair cells, which make nerve signals and send them to the brain.

- The wider parts next to the canals, the *utricle* and *saccule chambers*, have more blobs with hairs in them.

- Gravity pulls these down, bending the hairs and making the hair cells produce nerve signals.

- The canals sense head movements while the chambers detect head position.

- But balance involves much more, including information from the eyes about what is upright and level, from the skin about whether the body is leaning, and from inside the muscles and joints about strains on them.

- The brain uses all this information to adjust muscles and keep us well-balanced.

HOW WE HEAR

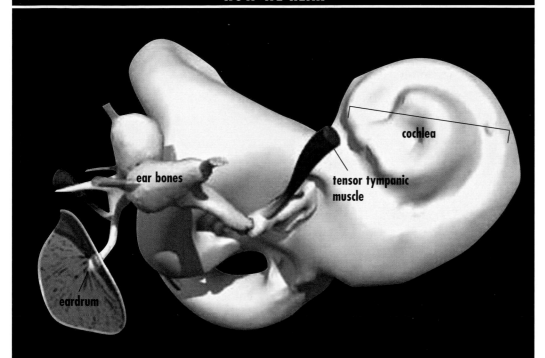

cochlea

ear bones

tensor tympanic muscle

eardrum

1 Sound waves approach as invisible ripples of high and low air pressure.

2 Outer ear flap funnels sound waves.

3 Ear canal carries them into the skull.

4 Eardrum vibrates as sound waves bounce off it.

5 Vibrations pass along row of three tiny bones, called *ossicles*.

6 Third ossicle makes the thin "window" of cochlea vibrate.

7 Vibrations pass into fluid inside cochlea, causing ripples.

8 Ripples shake 50–100 microhairs on each of 25,000 microscopic hair cells inside cochlea.

9 Hair cells make nerve signals when shaken.

10 Nerve signals pass along nerve fibers into the cochlear nerve.

11 Cochlear nerve is joined by vestibular nerve from balance parts.

12 Both nerves form the auditory nerve that carries nerve signals to brain.

PITCH

Sound reaches us as waves of vibrations of the air. Higher sounds make the air vibrate more quickly than lower sounds.

- Pitch is the scale of a sound — whether it makes the air vibrate at a high or low frequency.

- Our ears can detect sounds from 25 to 20,000 vibrations per second.

- Dogs can detect much lower and higher sounds than human beings.

EAR MEASUREMENTS

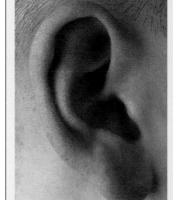

The ear canal leads from the outer ear to the eardrum. It is 0.78 in. long and slightly S-shaped.

Eardrum surface area 0.085 sq in. (about the size of the nail on the little finger).

Stirrup bone less than 0.2 in. long.

Cochlea spiral like a snail, with two 27° turns.

Cochlea 0.35 in. across at the wide end.

Cochlea straightened out would stretch 1.4 in.

Semicircular canals each 0.6–0.78 in. long, curved into a C-shape.(for balance)

Semicircular canals each less than 0.04 in. wide.

LOUDNESS OF SOUNDS

Sound intensity (roughly the same as loudness or volume) is measured in units called *decibels*, dB.

0 dB Total silence

10 dB Limit of human hearing

20 dB Watch ticking

30 dB Whisper

40 dB Quiet talking, distant traffic

50 dB Normal talking

60 dB Normal television volume

70 dB Traffic on city street, vacuum cleaner

80 dB Alarm clock ringing, nearby truck

90 dB Heavy traffic on highway, music at a concert

100 dB Chainsaw, construction drill

DAMAGE CONTROL

Some sounds are too loud for us to hear comfortably. We put our hands over our ears to try to protect our ears.

- Sounds above 90 dB, especially if high-pitched, can damage hearing.

- Many places have laws controlling noise, like factories, airports and music clubs.

NOSE AND TONGUE

Smell and taste are called *chemosenses*. This means the nose and tounge detect chemical substances—tiny particles too small to see. The nose reacts to particles called *odorants* floating in the air. The tongue detects particles called *flavorants* in foods and drinks. Both these senses are very useful, since they can warn us of danger, but they also give us plenty of pleasure.

The nasal and oral chambers— nose and mouth—form the front lower quarter of the head, each shaped by the skull and jaw bones around it.

FAST TRACK SIGNALS

Nerve signals about smell take a different route through the brain, compared to signals from other senses.

They pass through the part of brain called the *limbic system*, that is involved in feelings and emotions. This is why a strong smell brings back powerful memories and feelings.

• See pages 20–21 for information on THE BRAIN.

INSIDE THE NOSE

Nostrils
Two holes, each leading to one side of the nasal chamber.

Nasal cartilages
Curved sheets of cartilage forming the sticking-out part of the nose.

Nasal chamber
The air space inside the nose, roughly below the inner sides of the eyes.

Septum
Flat sheet of cartilage dividing the two halves of the nasal chamber.

Turbinates
Shelf-like ridges on each outer side of the nasal chamber.

Olfactory patch
Fuzzy-looking area inside the top of each half of the nasal chamber that detects smells.

LOCK AND KEY

Experts are still not exactly sure how smell and taste work. The main idea is the *lock and key theory*.

• Microscopic sense cells for both smell and taste are called *hair cells*, and have many tiny hairs sticking out, known as *cilia*.

• These hairs are coated with thousands of different-shaped receptors, or "landing pads".

A rose produces a particular smell particle that our nose can recognize.

• Each type of smell or flavor particle has its own particular shape.

• Particles try to fit in all the receptors on the hairs, but only fit into certain receptors of the same shape, like a key fitting into a lock.

• When a particle fits into a receptor, the hair cell sends a nerve signal to the brain.

• The brain works out the smell or taste from the overall pattern of nerve signals it receives.

MICRO-DETAILS: THE NOSE

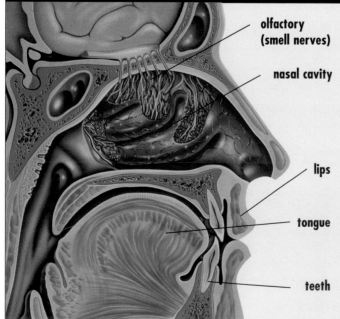

olfactory (smell nerves)

nasal cavity

lips

tongue

teeth

• The olfactory patch in the top of the nasal chamber is about the size of a thumbnail.

• Each olfactory patch has 10 million smell hair cells.

• Each smell hair cell has 10–20 micro-hairs sticking down from it.

• All the micro-hairs from one nose, joined end to end, would stretch over 109 yards.

• The micro-hairs stick into the sticky slimy mucus that lines the inside of the nasal chamber, inside the nose.

• Odorant particles floating in air seep into the slimy mucus coating the inside of the nasal chamber.

• They then come into contact with the micro-hairs.

• A single smell hair cell lives for about 30 days and is then replaced.

• Over many years, some smell hair cells die but are not replaced. Younger people have a more sensitive sense of smell than older people.

MICRO-DETAILS: THE TONGUE

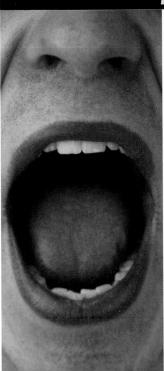

The tip, sides, and rear of the tongue have about 10,000 tiny taste buds, too small to see.

- Most taste buds are around and between the little lumps on the tongue, called *papillae*.

- Each taste bud is shaped like a tiny onion and contains about 25 taste receptor cells.

- Each taste receptor smell has about 10 short microhairs sticking up from it.

- The microhairs stick through a hole called a *taste pore*, at the top of the taste bud, onto the tongue's surface.

- Flavorant particles in foods and drinks seep into the saliva covering the tongue and come into contact with the microhairs.

- A single taste receptor cell lives for about 10 days and is then replaced.

- Over many years, some taste receptor cells die but are not replaced. So younger people have more sensitive taste than older people.

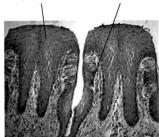

papillae   taste bud

A close up view of a taste bud.

HOW MANY?

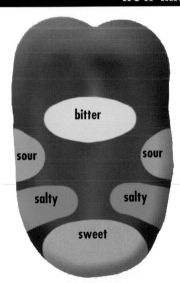

bitter

sour   sour

salty   salty

sweet

We sense four different basic flavors on the tongue, sweet, salty, sour, and bitter.

- While there may be larger groupings of certain taste buds, we can taste all favors all over the tongue. The "tongue map" (on right) was disproved in 1974.

- There are no taste buds on the main middle part of the tongue's upper surface or underneath the tongue.

NOSE AND MEMORY

With practice, most people could probably tell apart up to 10,000 different smells, odors, scents, and fragrances.

However, this depends on having a good memory as well as a sensitive nose.

SNIFF SNIFF

The nasal chamber inside the nose makes up to one litre of slimy mucus every day. Most we sniff in and swallow, some we blow out.

NOT ALL IT SEEMS

Food is less appetizing if we have a cold. The nose is full of mucus, hindering scent, and food seems less "tasty." In fact, it is less "smelly."

When we taste a meal, it is not only taste at work.

- Smells from food in the mouth float up, around the back of the roof of the mouth, into the nose.

- Here they are sensed by the nose in the usual way.

- Touch sensors in the gums and cheeks and on the tongue tell us about the food, too.

- These touch sensors detect if the food is hot or cold, hard or soft, or rough or smooth.

- Enjoying a meal involves taste, smell, and touch.

The tongue is the body's most flexible muscle.

It has twelve parts of muscles inside it, and it goes from long and thin, poking out, to short and wide at the back of the mouth, in less than a second.

In addition to taste, the tongue:

Helps in eating
- Moves food around inside the mouth to chew it well.
- Separates a smaller lump of food from the whole chewed mouthful, for swallowing.
- Cleans food off the teeth and lips.

Touches the lips
- Moistening the lips helps them seal together well.
- Stopping drool.

Communicates
- Changes shape while speaking to make words sound clear.
- Helps to make other sounds for communication, like whistles, hisses, and clicks.

T O N G U E
TWISTER

Usually we don't have to think about talking. The words just come out of our mouth.

When we try to say a tongue twister, we realize how difficult it can be for the brain and the tongue to work together. Try these!

- Which wristwatches are Swiss wristwatches?

- A skunk sat on a stump and thunk the stump stunk, but the stump thunk the skunk stunk.

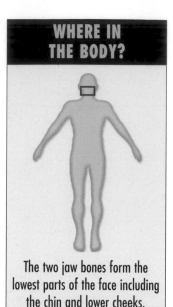

The two jaw bones form the lowest parts of the face including the chin and lower cheeks.

TEETH AND JAW

Teeth are the hardest parts of the whole body. We use them hundreds of times each day as we bite and chew. But they are the only body parts that cannot try to heal themselves if damaged or diseased. Not only do teeth break down the food we eat into smaller pieces, but they also work with the tongue to help us speak.

WHAT TEETH DO

Bite small pieces of large items of food.

Crush food into softer pieces.

Chew these into even softer pieces for easier swallowing.

NUMBERS OF TEETH

Baby, milk, or deciduous:
8 incisors
4 canines
8 premolars
Total: 20 in full set
Baby teeth are important because they help the adult teeth to grow into the correct shape.

Adult or permanent:
8 incisors
4 canines
8 premolars
12 molars
Total: 32 in full set

• See page 50–51
STAGES OF LIFE

TOOTH NAMES AND SHAPES

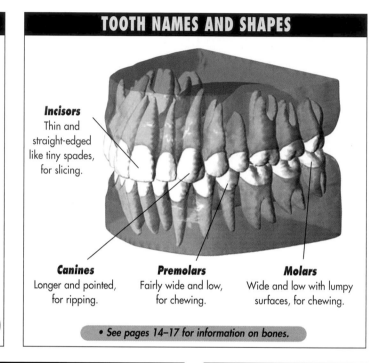

Incisors
Thin and straight-edged like tiny spades, for slicing.

Canines
Longer and pointed, for ripping.

Premolars
Fairly wide and low, for chewing.

Molars
Wide and low with lumpy surfaces, for chewing.

• See pages 14–17 for information on bones.

JAWS AND CHEWING

- The upper jaw bone is called the *maxilla*.

- The lower jaw bone is called the *mandible*.

- The mandible is the largest and strongest bone of the face.

- The mandible has some of the hardest, toughest bone in the body.

- One of the main chewing muscles is the *temporalis*, which runs from the temple (side of the head above the ear) to the lower side of the lower jaw.

- Another main chewing muscle is the *masseter*, which runs from the cheekbone to the lower side of the lower jaw.

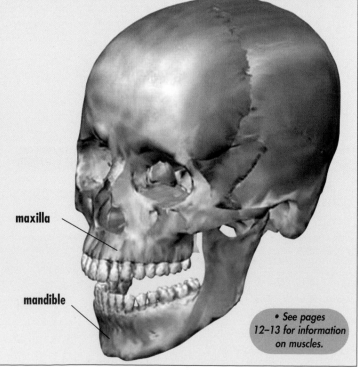

maxilla

mandible

• See pages 12–13 for information on muscles.

TWO ROOFS

The roof of the mouth has two main parts.

- The front part behind the nose is called the *hard palate*.

- It is formed by a backward-facing curved plate of the upper jaw bone (*maxilla*) plus part of another skull bone behind this, the *palatine bone*.

- The rear part above the back of the mouth is the *soft palate*.

- This is made mainly of muscles, cartilage (*gristle*) and fibers.

- It can bend up as a lump of food is pushed to the back of the mouth for swallowing.

PARTS OF A TOOTH

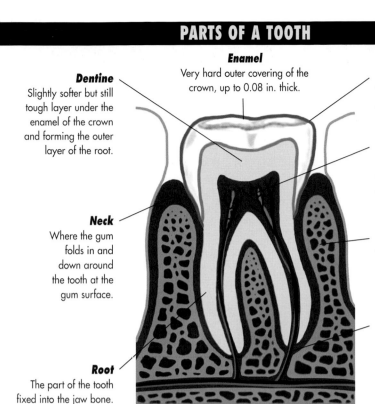

Enamel
Very hard outer covering of the crown, up to 0.08 in. thick.

Dentine
Slightly softer but still tough layer under the enamel of the crown and forming the outer layer of the root.

Crown
The part of the tooth above the gum.

Dental pulp
Soft innermost layer of the tooth, made mainly of blood vessels and nerve ends.

Neck
Where the gum folds in and down around the tooth at the gum surface.

Cementum
The "living glue" that sticks the tooth's root into the jaw.

Root canal
Small tunnel-like hole at base of root, where the blood vessels and nerves go from the jaw bone into the pulp.

Root
The part of the tooth fixed into the jaw bone.

PLAQUE DANGER

- All mouths are full of bacteria, although not all are harmful.

- Without proper brushing, bacteria will form on the hard enamel of the teeth.

- The bacteria multiply and form a film over the enamel. This is called *plaque*.

- Sugary foods help the plaque stick on to the tooth enamel.

- Sugar will also make the plaque produce acid, which eats into the tooth enamel.

- The acid makes tiny holes in the enamel. These get bigger and are called *cavities*.

- The tooth does not hurt until the acid reaches the nerves. By then, the cavity is already there.

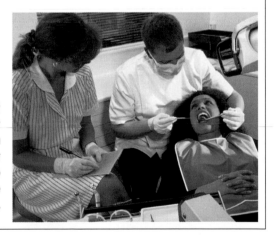

A dentist checks that your teeth are healthy and that no cavities are developing.

FALLING OUT, GROWING IN

Teeth	When baby teeth appear (months)	When adult teeth appear (years)
1st incisors	6–12	6–8
2nd incisors	9–15	7–9
Canines	14–20	9–12
1st premolars	15–20	10–12
2nd premolars	24–30	10–12
1st molars	–	6–7
2nd molars	–	11–13
3rd molars	–	18–21

FUNNY NAMES

- Eye teeth are called *canines*.

- Wisdom teeth are the rear-most molars, not appearing until a person is grown up and supposedly more experienced and wiser than when a child.

- In some people the wisdom teeth never grow above the gum.

FACTS ABOUT SALIVA

We could not chew and swallow without saliva. It would be very difficult to eat.

Chewing
- It moistens food so it is easier to chew.

- The moist food can be formed into a lump that slips down easily when swallowed.

- Our taste sensors do not work as well when food is dry, so saliva gives dry food its taste.

Enzymes
- Chemicals called *enzymes* in saliva begin to digest the food as it is chewed, especially starchy foods like potato, bread, rice, and pasta.

Hygiene
- Saliva washes away small particles of food and helps to keep the mouth clean.

- See page 38–39 for information on digestion.

HOW SALIVA IS MADE

Saliva is made in six salivary glands around the face.

- The *parotid glands* are below and to the front of each ear.

- The *submandibular glands* are in the angle of the lower jaw.

- The *sublingual glands* are in the floor of the mouth below the tongue.

- Together the six glands make a total of about 3 pints of saliva each day.

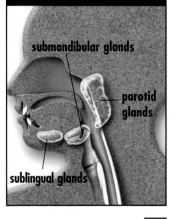

submandibular glands

parotid glands

sublingual glands

LUNGS AND BREATHING

The body's breathing or respiratory system obtains the vital substance oxygen from the air around us. Oxygen is needed to take part in the body chemistry that breaks apart blood sugar, called *glucose*, releasing its energy to power almost every body process and action. The main parts of the system are the lungs, reached by the series of airways leading down through the nose, throat, and windpipe.

• See pages 26–27 for information on the nose.

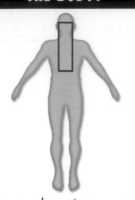

Air enters the respiratory system through the nose or mouth and travels down the windpipe to the lungs in the chest.

SIZE AND SHAPE OF THE LUNGS

- Each lung is shaped almost like a cone.

- The upper point, or *apex*, reaches slightly higher than the collar bone across the top of the chest to the shoulder.

- The wide base sits on the dome-shaped main breathing muscle, the *diaphragm*, which is roughly level with the bottom of the breastbone but curves down to the bottom ribs around the sides.

- The left lung has two main parts, or *lobes*, and a scooped-out shape where the heart fits.

- The right lung has three lobes and is on average about one-fifth bigger than the left lung.

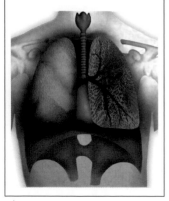

TOTAL BREATHING

- Volume of air passing through the lungs in a year: 1,056,000 gallons.

- Number of breaths in a lifetime: about 500 million.

AIR SPEEDS

Air is expelled from our lungs at different rates.

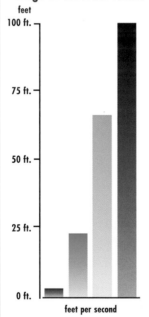

feet

100 ft.

75 ft.

50 ft.

25 ft.

0 ft.

feet per second

Normal breathing –
6.5 feet per second

Fast breathing –
23 feet per second

Coughing –
65 feet per second

Sneeze –
96 feet per second

AIR AND BREATHING RATES

These are average volumes for an adult man. For women, the amounts are about one-quarter less.

All the air in the lungs when fully breathed in:	12.6 pints
Air in the lungs left after completely breathing out:	2.5 pints
Air between breathing out normally, and breathing out forcefully and completely:	2 pints
Air breathed in and out at rest:	17 fl. oz.
Extra air when breathing in very forcefully:	7 pints
Normal breathing rate at rest:	15 in-and-out per minute
Breathing rate after great activity:	50 per minute
Amount of air breathed in and out after great activity:	6.3 pints

- **The amount of air going into and coming out of lungs per minute varies from 1.9 gallons at rest to 40 gallons after strenuous activity.**

• See page 32 for the heart rate during exercise.

HOW AIR CHANGES

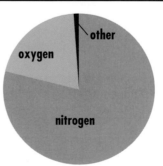

oxygen | other | nitrogen

oxygen | other | nitrogen

Fresh air breathed in

79% nitrogen

20% oxygen

0.03% carbon dioxide

Stale air breathed out

79% nitrogen

16% oxygen

4% carbon dioxide

Air passes through a series of chambers and tubes on its way to deep in the lungs.

The total length of all the air tubes in the lungs joined end to end is about 31 miles.

• See page 54 for information on the tonsils.

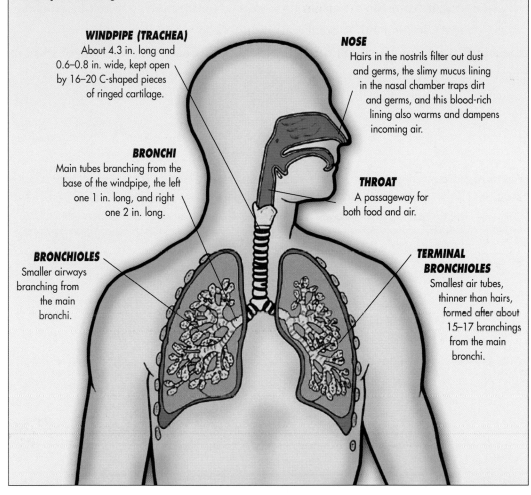

WINDPIPE (TRACHEA)
About 4.3 in. long and 0.6–0.8 in. wide, kept open by 16–20 C-shaped pieces of ringed cartilage.

NOSE
Hairs in the nostrils filter out dust and germs, the slimy mucus lining in the nasal chamber traps dirt and germs, and this blood-rich lining also warms and dampens incoming air.

BRONCHI
Main tubes branching from the base of the windpipe, the left one 1 in. long, and right one 2 in. long.

THROAT
A passageway for both food and air.

BRONCHIOLES
Smaller airways branching from the main bronchi.

TERMINAL BRONCHIOLES
Smallest air tubes, thinner than hairs, formed after about 15–17 branchings from the main bronchi.

FAIR EXCHANGE

The places where oxygen is taken into the body are tiny bubble-shaped spaces deep in the lungs, called *alveoli*.

- Alveoli are bunched at the end of the smallest airways, the *terminal bronchioles*.

- There are 250-300 million alveoli in each lung.

- Breathing not only takes in oxygen, it also gets rid of the waste product carbon dioxide, which would soon poison the body if it was not expelled.

Spread out flat, all the alveoli from both lungs would cover a tennis court.

BREATHING AND SPEECH

Air passing out of the lungs has a useful extra effect — speech.

- There are nine pieces of cartilage in the larynx.

- Front ridge of the thyroid cartilage forms the "Adam's apple" that males and females have, but is more noticeable in males.

- About 19 muscles of the larynx alter the length of the vocal cords, called *vocal folds*, to make the sounds of speech.

- The vocal cords are about 0.2 in. longer in men than women, giving a deeper voice.

- Average pitch of male vocal cords: 120 Hz (vibrations per second).

- Average pitch of female vocal cords: 220 Hz (vibrations per second).

- Average pitch of child's vocal cords: 260 Hz (vibrations per second).

THE VOICEBOX

Above the voicebox is the leaf-shaped flap of epiglottis cartilage. When food is swallowed, this folds down over the entrance to the voicebox to prevent food entering the airway and causing choking.

THE HEART

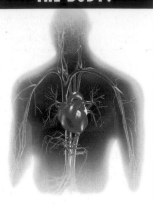

The heart is between the lungs. It tips slightly to the left side, which is why people think it is on the left side of the body.

In the center of your chest, below a thin layer of skin, muscle, and bone, sits your heart. This simple, yet essential, pump carries blood to and from your body's billions of cells nonstop, day and night. During an average lifetime of 70 years, the heart beats 2.5 billion times. Without the heart's second-by-second collection and delivery service, your cells—and your body—would die.

THE HEART'S JOB

The right and left sides of the heart work side-by-side like two pumps.

Every time the heart contracts, or beats, the right side pumps oxygen-poor blood back to the lungs to pick up oxygen, and the left side pumps oxygen-rich blood from the lungs out into the body.

PULSE RATE (HEARTBEATS) PER MINUTE

The number of heartbeats per minute is called the *pulse rate*. The resting heart rate changes throughout our lives. When we exercise, our heart needs to supply more oxygen to our bodies, so it pumps harder and faster.

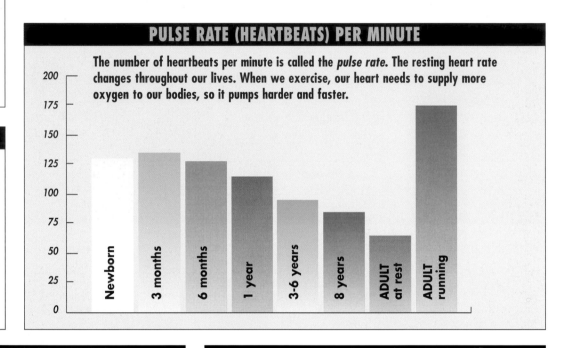

Chart values: 200, 175, 150, 125, 100, 75, 50, 25, 0

Categories: Newborn, 3 months, 6 months, 1 year, 3-6 years, 8 years, ADULT at rest, ADULT running

PHYSICAL CHARACTERISTICS

The heart is about the size of its owner's clenched fist. As you grow from a child into an adult, your heart will grow at the same rate as your clenched fist.

Average heart weight male:	**10.5 oz.**	Size:	Length:	**4.7 in.**
Average heart weight female:	**8.8 oz.**		Width:	**3.1–3.5 in.**
			Front to back:	**2.3 in.**

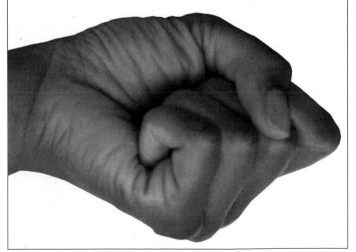

WHAT MAKES THE HEART BEAT?

At the top of the heart is a tiny area called the *sinoatrial node*. It sends out electrical signals that make the cells in the heart wall contract.

THE HEART'S OWN BLOOD SUPPLY

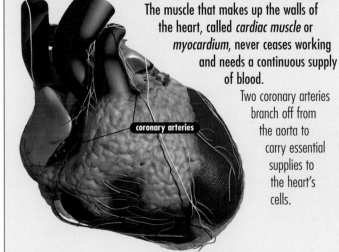

coronary arteries

The muscle that makes up the walls of the heart, called *cardiac muscle* or *myocardium*, never ceases working and needs a continuous supply of blood.

Two coronary arteries branch off from the aorta to carry essential supplies to the heart's cells.

THE HEART (VIEWED FROM THE FRONT)

Superior (upper) vena cava

Sinoatrial node

Right atrium

Aorta

Pulmonary artery

Left atrium

Pulmonary veins

Pulmonary valve

Mitral valve

Pericardium

Tricuspid valve

Septum

Left ventricle

Inferior (lower) vena cava

Right ventricle

Heartstrings

Muscular wall of cardiac (heart) muscle

PARTS OF THE HEART

Aorta
The largest artery in the body. It is about the diameter of a garden hose.

Atrium
One of the two small upper chambers in the heart that receives blood from the veins and passes it to the ventricles below.

Heartstrings
Cords that hold the valve in place between the atrium and the ventricle.

Inferior Vena Cava
A large vein that collects blood from the lower half of the body.

Pericardium
The tough outer covering of the heart.

Septum
Muscular wall that divides the left and right sides of the heart.

Superior Vena Cava
A large vein which collects blood from the upper half of the body.

Valve
A sort of door that only opens one way to let blood through, but stops it flowing backwards. The heart has four valves: the tricuspid, pulmonary, mitral, and aortic valves.

Ventricle
One of the two large lower chambers in the heart that receives blood from the atrium above and passes it out into the arteries.

HOW THE HEART WORKS

Dotted lines represent oxygen-poor blood

•••• 1) Blood flows in from the body to the right atrium through the superior and inferior vena cavas. It is known as oxygen-poor blood because the body has taken and used the oxygen that the blood was carrying.

•••• 2) The right atrium pumps the blood through the tricuspid valve into the right ventricle.

•••• 3) The right ventricle pumps the blood through the pulmonary valve into the pulmonary artery and off into the lungs.

Inside the lungs

4) As the blood travels through the lungs, it releases waste gases and picks up oxygen.

Dashed lines represent oxygen-rich blood

- - - 5) The blood flows from the lungs into the left atrium through the pulmonary veins.

- - - 6) The left atrium pumps the blood into the left ventricle.

- - - 7) The left ventricle pumps the blood through the aortic valve into the aorta and off around the body.

CIRCULATORY SYSTEM

Something that circulates goes around and around, and that's exactly what your blood does inside your body. Pumped by your heart, your blood flows around a network of pipes and tubes called *blood vessels*, on a nonstop, never-ending journey around your body. The blood vessels, together with the heart and blood, all make up the circulatory system.

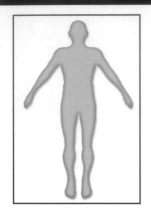

Blood vessels reach every tiny part of your body from the top of your head to the ends of your fingers and toes.

- Some parts have much fewer blood vessels than others, such as the tough, tapering tendons at the ends of muscles, which have more than 10 times fewer blood vessels than the muscle itself.

- Only a few small body parts have no blood vessels at all, for example, the lens of the eye.

DIFFERENT NAMES

The circulatory system is also called the cardiovascular system.

- *Cardio* comes from the ancient Greek word *kardia* that means *heart*.

- *Vascular* comes from the Latin word *vas* that means *vessel*.

- The vessels leading to and from each body part are known as its *vascular supply*.

BLUE AND RED

Blood that has a lot of oxygen in it is red. When the body has used the oxygen, the blood becomes blue.

- Arteries carry blood from the heart, but not all of this blood is high in oxygen.

- The pulmonary arteries from the right side of the heart to the lungs carry blood low in oxygen.

- Similarly, veins carry blood to the heart, but not all of this blood is low in oxygen.

- The pulmonary veins from the lungs to the left side of the heart carry blood high in oxygen.

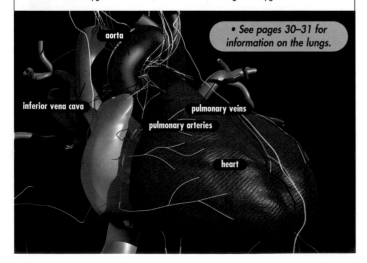

aorta

inferior vena cava

pulmonary veins

pulmonary arteries

heart

• See pages 30–31 for information on the lungs.

MAIN VEINS AND ARTERIES

Exercise pumps the blood around the body faster.

Veins

- The main vein bringing blood from the head, arms, and upper body back to the heart is called the *superior vena cava*.

- The main vein bringing blood from the lower body, hips, and legs back the heart is called the *inferior vena cava*.

- Both these main veins are about 1.2 in. wide.

- Blood flows very slowly through them, at only 0.04 in. per second.

- At any single moment, these main veins contain one-tenth of all the body's blood.

Arteries

- The body's main artery is the *aorta*, carrying blood from the left side of the heart to all body parts.

- The aorta is 15.7 in. long and arches up, over, and behind the heart, inside the chest.

- The aorta's width is about 0.98 in.

- Its walls are 0.1 in. thick.

- Blood surges through the aorta at about 1.18 in. per second.

• See pages 36–37 for information on BLOOD.

NAMING THE PARTS

Most arteries and veins are named from the body parts they supply.

Cerebral vessels in the head.

• See pages 20–21 for information on THE BRAIN.

• See pages 38–39 for information on the stomach.

Coronary arteries carry blood to the heart's muscular walls, and are named because their branching shape looks like a crown (*corona*) around the heart.

Hepatic artery and vein for the liver.

Renal artery and vein for the kidney.

Gastric artery and vein for the stomach.

Iliac artery and vein to the leg.

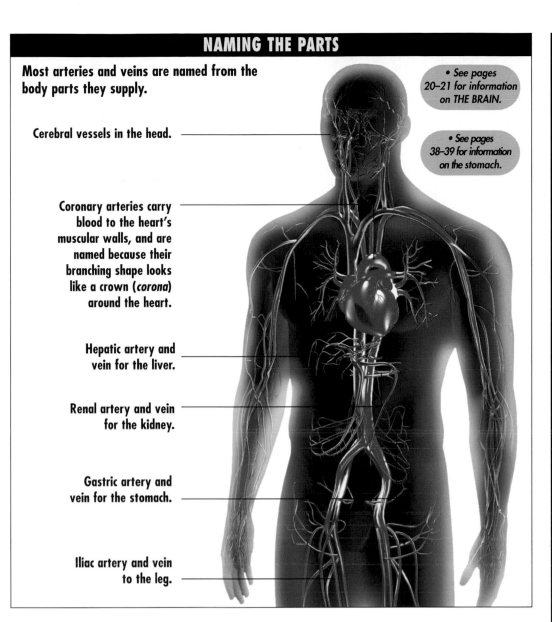

TYPES OF BLOOD VESSELS

Arteries
• Carry blood away from the heart.

• Thick, muscular walls to cope with the surge of high pressure as blood is forced from the heart with each heartbeat.

• Take blood to the body's main parts or organs.

• Divide and become thinner forming arterioles.

Arterioles
• Smaller and shorter than arteries.

• Muscles in the walls can tighten to make the arterioles smaller, or relax and make them wider to control amount of blood flowing through.

• Divide and become narrower, forming capillaries.

Capillaries
• The smallest blood vessels, very short and too thin to see without a microscope.

• Walls are so thin (just one cell thick) that nutrients and useful substances can pass from the blood inside, through the walls to cells and tissues around.

• Thin walls also allow wastes and unwanted substances to pass from cells and tissues around, into the blood, to be taken away.

• Join together to form venules.

Venules
• Thin-walled and very flexible.

• Collect blood from within each main body part.

• Join together, forming veins.

Veins
• Wide, with thin, floppy walls.

• Have pocket-like valves sticking out from their walls, to make sure blood flows the correct way.

• Carry blood from main body parts back to the heart.

BLOOD VESSEL CHART

Blood vessel	Typical diameter across (in.)	Wall thickness (in.)	Typical length (in.)	Blood pressure inside (blood emerging from heart = max 100)
Arteries	0.2	0.4	6	90
Arterioles	0.019	0.0007	0.2	60
Capillaries	0.00003	0.00004	0.02	30
Venules	0.0007	0.000001	0.1	20
Veins	0.6	0.019	6	10

JOURNEY TIMES

The journey time for any tiny drop of blood depends on its route around the circulatory system.

• A short trip from the heart's right side to the lungs and straight back to the heart's left side can take less than 10 seconds.

• A long trip from the heart's left side all the way down through the body and legs to the toes, then all the way back the heart's right side, can take more than a minute.

• See pages 32–33 for information on THE HEART.

LENGTH AND AREA

• If all the body's blood vessels could be taken out and joined end to end, they would stretch about 62,137 m., which is two and a half times around the world.

• If all the capillaries were ironed flat their total surface area would be about half a soccer field.

BLOOD

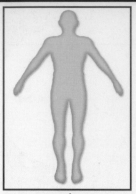

P umped by the heart, blood flows through tubes, called *blood vessels*, to every part of the body. Blood carries useful substances like oxygen and nutrients to all body parts. It also collects wastes and unwanted substances that are removed mainly by the kidneys. But the blood does much much more than just delivering oxygen and picking up waste.

At any single moment about ⅙ of all the body's blood is in the arteries, almost ¾ is in the veins, and less than 1/20 is in the tiny capillaries inside body parts or organs.

HOW MUCH?

The amount of blood in the body depends mainly on body size.

- On average, blood is 1/12 of the body's total weight.

- This is slightly less in women compared to men.

- Most women naturally have more fatty tissue than men, which has less blood supply compared to other body parts.

- Also, most women naturally have less muscle tissue than men, which has more blood supply compared to other body parts.

- An average adult female has 8.4–10.5 pints of blood.

- An average adult male has 10.5–12.6 pints of blood.

- For people of average weight and build, the volume of blood is about 1.8 fl. oz. per lb. of body weight.

• See pages 12–13 for information on muscles.

BLOOD FLOW THROUGH BODY PARTS

In general, busier body parts need more blood supply.

- When a body part is active, changes occur in the blood vessels in order to supply it with more blood.

- The muscles in the walls of the small blood vessels, called *arterioles*, relax.

- This allows more blood to flow through them to the part they supply.

- The width of the arterioles is controlled mainly by signals from the brain sent along nerves.

- The hormone *adrenaline* also affects the width of the arterioles.

• See pages 34–35 for information on the CIRCULATORY SYSTEM.

BLOOD TYPES

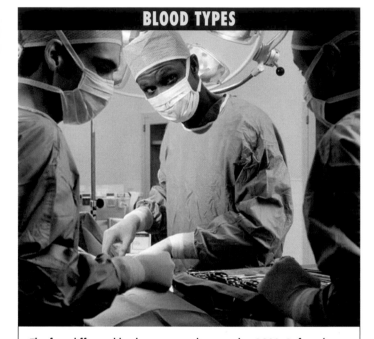

The four different blood types were discovered in 1900. Before this, blood transfusions had a high rate of failure. Today, we realize it is vital to know the blood types of the donor and the patient in order for blood to be used safely.

- Certain kinds or groups of blood, when mixed together, may form clumps or clots.

- This can be dangerous during a blood transfusion, when blood is given or donated by one person, to be put into another person, the recipient .

- ABO is the system for testing blood for its group. A person can be either A, B, AB, or O.

- A person with type O is a universal donor, whose blood can be given to almost anyone. A person with type AB is a universal recipient, who can receive blood from almost anyone.

Blood type of person	Can donate blood to	Can receive blood from
A	A, AB	A, O
B	B, AB	B, O
AB	AB	A, B, AB, O
O	A, B, AB, O	O

RED BLOOD CELLS

Red blood cells carry oxygen around the body.

- Red blood cells are among the most numerous cells, with 25,000 billion in an average person.

- They are also among the smallest cells, each one just 7 microns, 0.000028 in., across and 2 microns thick.

- Each red cell is shaped like a doughnut without the hole poked completely though.

- A red cell's color is due to the substance *haemoglobin*.

- Haemoglobin joins or attaches to oxygen and carries it around the body.

- Each red cell contains 250 million tiny molecules of haemoglobin.

- Each red blood cell lives for three or four months, then dies and is broken apart.

- This means about 3 million red blood cells die every second — and the same number of new ones are made.

- Red blood cells, like white blood cells and platelets, are made in the jelly-like marrow inside bones.

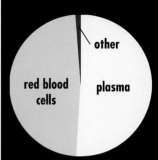

WHAT IS IN BLOOD?

Blood is mostly made up of plasma and red blood cells. White blood cells and platelets make up a tiny proportion of the total.

Plasma
- Forms just over half of blood by volume.
- Pale, tan color.
- Over nine-tenths is water.
- Contains many dissolved substances, such as glucose, hormones, body salts, and minerals, unwanted wastes such as urea, disease-fighting antibodies, and dozens of others.

Red blood cells
- Nearly half of all blood.
- Also called *erythrocytes*.
- Carry oxygen from the lungs all around the body.
- Pick up carbon dioxide to take back to the lungs for removal.

White blood cells
- Form less than $\frac{1}{100}$ of blood.
- Also called *leucocytes*.
- Attack, disable, and kill invading germs.
- Engulf or eat waste bits such as pieces of old, broken-down cells.

Platelets
- Form less than $\frac{1}{100}$ of blood.
- Also called *thrombocytes*.
- Are not so much whole living microscopic cells, but parts or fragments of cells.
- Help blood to clot (*thrombose*) to seal cuts and wounds.

BLOOD FLOW AT REST AND AT WORK

Part of the body	Flow in pints per minute	
	At rest	During hard exercise
Heart	0.5	1.5
Kidneys	2.5	1.2
Main muscles	2.1	25.4
Skin	0.8	4.2
Stomach, intestines	2.9	1.2
Brain	1.5	1.5

Only the brain's blood flow stays the same no matter how active the body is, from running a fast race to fast asleep.

IN ONE DROP OF BLOOD

A pinhead-sized drop of blood, contains:

- 5 million red blood cells.
- 5,000 white blood cells.
- 250,000 platelets.

If a person is ill, the number of germ-fighting white cells in blood may rise from 5,000 to 25,000.

DIGESTION

Your body needs fuel to function. Food gives you the energy to move about, walk and run, and keep your inside processes going, like heartbeat and breathing. But food gives you more than energy. It provides nutrients for growth, making newer and bigger body parts, repairing old worn-out ones, and staying healthy, too. The parts of the body specialized to take in and break down foods into tiny pieces form the *digestive system*.

WHERE IN THE BODY?

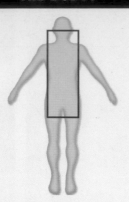

The digestive system starts at the mouth and ends at the anus. Most of its main parts, the stomach and intestines, are in the abdomen (lower half of the main body).

APPENDIX: A PUZZLING PART

The appendix is a finger-sized part of the body, branching from the start of the large intestine.

- It is a dead end, with its tip sealed.

- Hollow inside.

- Varies in length from 2–6 in.

- Seems to have no important task in digestion (or anything else).

The appendix may swell up with "stuck" food and germs, causing *appendicitis* with severe pain in the lower right abdomen.

FOOD'S JOURNEY

Part of tract	Length (in.)	Time spent by food
Mouth	3.9	Up to 1 minute
Throat	3.9	2–4 seconds
Esophagus	10	2–5 seconds
Stomach	10	3–6 hours
Small intestine	228	2–4 hours
Large intestine	60	5–10 hours
Rectum	7.8	5–8 hours

RECYCLING

- The digestive system makes more than 2.6 gallons of digestive juices each day.

- Most of the water in these juices is taken back into the body by the large intestine.

- Only about 0.3 fl. oz. is lost in the wastes from the system.

- The digestive system recycles $^{99}/_{100}$ of its water.

STOMACH

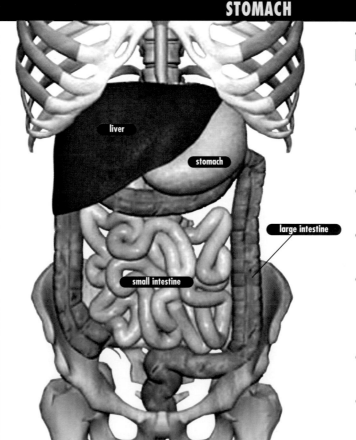

liver
stomach
large intestine
small intestine

The stomach is a J-shaped bag behind the left lower ribs.

- Measures about 12 in. around its longer side.

- Has thick muscle layers in its walls that squirm and squeeze to mash the food inside.

- Average amount of food and drink contents is 3 pints.

- Lining makes about 3 pints of gastric juices each day.

- Gastric juices include hydrochloric acid and digestive chemicals, called *enzymes*—pepsin attacks proteins in food, and lipase attacks fats.

- Takes in or absorbs few nutrients, including sugars.

- Lining also makes thick slimy mucus, to protect the stomach's gastric juices from digesting itself.

THE DIGESTIVE TRACT

The digestive system includes the digestive tract described here, and also parts that work along with this, including the liver and pancreas. The digestive tract is the passageway for food.

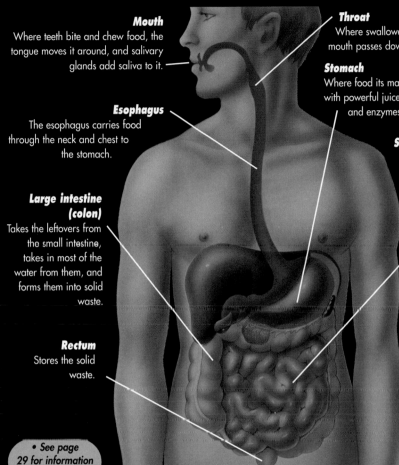

Mouth
Where teeth bite and chew food, the tongue moves it around, and salivary glands add saliva to it.

Esophagus
The esophagus carries food through the neck and chest to the stomach.

Large intestine (colon)
Takes the leftovers from the small intestine, takes in most of the water from them, and forms them into solid waste.

Rectum
Stores the solid waste.

• See page 29 for information on saliva.

Throat
Where swallowed food from the mouth passes down to the esophagus.

Stomach
Where food its mashed and mixed with powerful juices containing acids and enzymes.

Small intestine
Receives part-digested, soupy food from the stomach, adds more juices and enzymes to it, and absorbs the various nutrients.

• See pages 42–43 for LIVER AND PANCREAS.

Anus
The last part of the passageway, a ring of muscle that relaxes to let out the solid waste.

SMALL INTESTINE

- Average width is 1.1–1.3 in.
- Has three main parts: duodenum (10 in.), jejunum (88 in.) and ileum (118 in.).
- Receives digestive juices from the pancreas and liver.
- Inner surface has many folds, called *plicae*.
- On these folds are tiny finger-like shapes, *villi*, about 0.4 in. long.
- All the villi joined end to end would stretch 248 miles.
- On each villus are even more microscopic finger-like shapes, *microvilli*.
- Plicae, villi, and microvilli greatly increase surface area of inside of small intestine, to about 6 12 sq yd., to absorb as many nutrients as possible from food.

There are about 500 million villi in the body.

PUSHING FOOD

- Without food inside, most of the digestive passageway is squeezed flat by the natural pressure inside the body.
- Food has to be pushed through the passageway by waves of muscle action in its walls, called *peristalsis*.

In the esophagus, peristalsis is so strong it works even if the body is upside down.

LEFTOVERS

- The average weight of solid waste is 5.2 oz. per day.
- The weight varies greatly, increasing with the amount of fiber in food.

Two-thirds water, about 3.5 oz.

One-ninth is dead microbes that live naturally in the large intestine and help with digestion.

One-ninth or more of the rest is undigested food, especially fiber.

One-ninth is rubbed-off parts of the digestive lining.

• See page 41 for information on FIBER.

LARGE INTESTINE

- Average width 2.3–2.7 in.
- First part is wider, the *caecum*, and has the appendix branching from it.
- Second part is the *ascending colon*, going up the right side of the abdomen.
- Third part is the *transverse colon*, across the top of the abdomen.
- Fourth part is the *sigmoid* (S-shaped) colon, on the lower left of the abdomen.
- Mainly takes back water and valuable body salts and minerals from leftover foods and wastes.

FOOD AND NUTRIENTS

Have you had plenty of lipids, complex carbohydrates, trace metallic elements, and cellulose today? These are all substances that your body needs to stay healthy, but their names are quite complicated. Usually, we call these substances, and everything else the body needs to take in every day, by a simpler name—food. However, in your food there are six main groups of substances which you may have heard about: proteins, carbohydrates, fats, vitamins, minerals, and fiber.

DIFFERENT SORTS OF FOOD

Food can be divided into groups. This can help us plan a balanced diet.

Yellow: meat and fish
Green: grains
Red: fruit and vegetables
Blue: dairy products
Orange: sugary foods

We should eat foods from each of these groups in order to stay healthy. We should choose more grains, fruit, and vegetables, and eat less sugary food.

MINERAL CHART

Iron
Needed for: red blood cells, skin, muscles, resisting stress, fighting disease

Calcium
Needed for: bones, teeth, nerves, heartbeat, blood clotting, kidneys

Sodium
Needed for: nerves and nerve signals, digestion, blood, chemical processes inside cells, kidneys

Magnesium
Needed for: heartbeat and rhythm, energy use

Iodine
Needed for: overall speed of body's chemical processes, making thyroid hormone

Zinc
Needed for: healthy immune system, wound healing, maintaining senses of smell and taste

DAILY NEEDS

For an average adult with a typical office job, daily needs are:

Carbohydrates   300 grams
(including 25 grams or more of fiber)

Proteins   50 grams

Fats   60 grams
(mostly from plant sources)

Vitamins, examples:
Vitamin C   0.06 gram
Vitamin K   0.00008 gram

Minerals, examples:
Calcium   1 gram
Iron   0.018 gram
Chloride   3.4 grams

CARBOHYDRATES

Carbohydrates are "energy foods."

- Broken down by digestion into smaller, simpler pieces, such as sugars.

- Taken in and used as the body's main source of energy, called *glucose* or *blood sugar*, for the life processes of all its microscopic cells.

- Also used for all muscle movements from heartbeat and breathing to fast running.

- Foods with plenty of carbohydrates are starchy or sweet, such as rice, wheat, barley, and other grains. Products made from these are pasta and bread. There are also many "starchy" vegetables, like potatoes and corn, and many sweet fruits like bananas and strawberries, as well as sugary items like candy and chocolate.

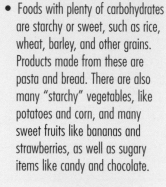

Bread is made from wheat, a good source of carbohydrates.

FATS AND OILS

Fats are used for both building and energy.

- Broken down by digestion into smaller, simpler pieces, called *lipids*.

- Foods with plenty of fats are usually fatty plant parts; including red meats; oily fish; eggs, milk, cheese, and other dairy products; and certain foods like avocados, olives, and peanuts.

- Taken in and used both for building parts, such as nerves, making and repairing parts of microscopic cells, and as energy that carbohydrates are lacking.

- Too much fat from animal sources (fatty red meats and processed foods, like burgers and salami) is linked to various health problems, such as heart disease and high blood pressure.

Fat is an important part of our diet, but we should get most of what we need from plant sources, such as olive oil.

PROTEINS

Foods rich in protein are sometimes called *building foods,* as they help to build our body parts.

- Broken down by digestion into smaller, simpler pieces called *amino acids.*

- Amino acids are taken in and built into the body's own proteins that make up the main structure of muscles, bones, skin, and most other parts.

- Foods with plenty of protein include all kinds of meats; poultry like chicken, fish, and eggs; dairy products like milk and cheese; and some plant foods like nuts, soybeans, and other beans and peas.

Dairy products such as cheese and sour cream are a good source of protein.

FIBER

Fiber is needed to help food pass through our body properly.

- Sometimes called *roughage.*
- Is not really broken down or digested by the body. It passes through the digestive tract largely unaltered.
- Needed to give food "bulk," so the intestines can grip it and make it move through them.
- Helps to satisfy hunger, reducing the temptation to eat too much.
- Reduces the risk of wastes being too small and hard and getting stuck, called *constipation.*

- Fiber also reduces risks of various intestinal diseases, including certain kinds of colon cancer.

Fresh fruit and vegetables are a good source of fiber, particularly if the the skins are eaten as well.

FIVE-A-DAY GUIDE

"Five-a-day" means five helpings, portions, or servings of fresh fruits or vegetables each day.

This should provide the body with enough of all the vitamins and minerals, as well as some energy and plenty of fiber.

Drinking a glass of fresh fruit juice counts as one portion of your "five-a-day" target.

VITAMINS

- Needed for various body processes to work, stay healthy, and ward off disease.

- Most are needed in small amounts, fractions of a gram per day.

- Have chemical names and also letters like A and B.

- The body can store some vitamins, but needs regular supplies of others.

- Eating a wide range of foods, especially fresh fruits and vegetables, should provide all the body's needs.

Snacking on fresh fruits and vegetables will help to meet your body's vitamin requirements.

MINERALS

- Needed for various body processes to work, stay healthy, and ward off disease.

- Most are needed in small amounts, fractions of a gram per day.

- Most are simple chemical substances, like iron, calcium, and sodium.

- The body can store some minerals but needs regular supplies of others.

- Eating a wide range of foods, especially fresh fruits and vegetables, should provide all the body's needs.

VITAMIN CHART

Vitamin A
Chemical name: *Carotene*

Needed for: eyes, skin, teeth, bones, general health

Vitamin B1
Chemical name: *Thiamine*

Needed for: brain, nerves, muscles, heart, energy use, general health

Vitamin B2
Chemical name: *Riboflavin*

Needed for: blood, eyes, skin, hair, nails, fighting disease, general health

Vitamin B3
Chemical name: *Nicotinic acid*

Needed for: energy use, controlling blood contents

Vitamin B6
Chemical name: *Pyridoxine*

Needed for: chemical processes inside cells, brain, skin, muscle, energy use, general health

Vitamin B12
Chemical name: *Cobalamin*

Needed for: blood, brain, nerves, growing, energy use, general health

Vitamin BF
Chemical name: *Folic acid*

Needed for: blood, digestion, growth

Vitamin C
Chemical name: *Ascorbic acid*

Needed for: teeth, gums, bones, blood, fighting disease, skin, general health

Vitamin D
Chemical name: *Cholecalciferol*

Needed for: bones, teeth, nerves, heart, others general health

Vitamin E
Chemical name: *Tocopherol*

Needed for: blood, cell processes, muscles, nerves, general health

Vitamin K
Chemical name: *Phylloquinone*

Needed for: blood clotting, general health

LIVER AND PANCREAS

The body can't digest food with just its digestive tract. The body also needs the liver and pancreas. These are next to the stomach and they are digestive glands, which means they make powerful substances to break down food in the intestines. Together with the digestive tract, the liver and pancreas make up the whole digestive system.

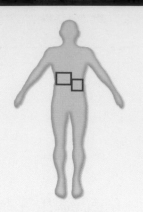

The liver is in the upper abdomen, behind the lower right ribs. The pancreas is in the upper left abdomen, behind the stomach.

WARM LIVER

The liver is so busy with chemical processes and tasks that it makes lots of heat.

- When the body is at rest and the muscles are still, the liver makes up to one-fifth of the body's total warmth.

- The heat from the liver isn't wasted. Blood spreads the heat all around the body.

See pages 34–35 for information on the CIRCULATORY SYSTEM.

GALL BLADDER AND BILE

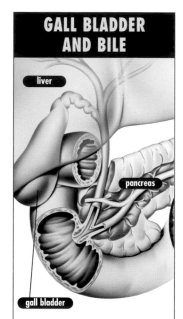

liver

pancreas

gall bladder

THE LIVER'S TASKS

The liver has more than 500 known tasks in the body, and probably more that haven't yet been discovered. Some of the main ones are:

- Breaking down nutrients and other substances from digestion brought direct to the liver from the small intestine.

- Storing vitamins for times when they may be lacking in food.

- Making bile, a digestive juice.

- If levels of blood sugar are too low, changing body starch back into blood sugar and releasing it.

- Breaking apart old, dead, worn-out red blood cells.

- Breaking down toxins and possibly harmful substances, like alcohol and poisons.

- Helping to control the amount of water in blood and body tissues.

- If levels of blood sugar are too high, changing this into body starch and storing it.

Alcohol is a toxins thatthe liver breaks down and makes harmless. Too much alcohol can overload the liver and cause a serious disease called *cirrhosis*.

The gall bladder is a small storage bag under the liver.

- It is 3.1 in. long and 1.1in. wide.

- Some of the bile fluid made in the liver is stored in the gall bladder.

- The gall bladder can hold up to 1.6 fl. oz. of bile.

- After a meal, bile pours from the liver along the main bile duct, and from the gall bladder along the cystic duct into the small intestine.

- Bile helps to digest the fats and oils in foods.

- The liver makes up to two pints of bile each day.

HOW THE PANCREAS WORKS

Fatty foods, such as fries, are broken apart by enzymes made in the pancreas.

- Pancreas has two main jobs.

- One is to make hormones.

- The other is to make digestive chemicals called *pancreatic juices.*

- These juices contain about 15 powerful enzymes that break apart many substances in foods, including proteins, carbohydrates, and fats.

- Pancreas makes about 3 pints of digestive juices daily.

- During a meal, these pass along the pancreatic duct tubes into the small intestine to digest foods there.

• See page 52 for information on hormones.

WHEN THINGS GO WRONG

A yellowish tinge to the skin and eyes is known as *jaundice*. It is often a sign of liver trouble.

Usually, the liver breaks down old red blood cells and gets rid of the coloring substance in bile fluid. If something goes wrong, the coloring substance builds up in blood and skin and causes jaundice.
Hepatitis, an infection of the liver, can cause jaundice.

UNUSUAL SUPPLY

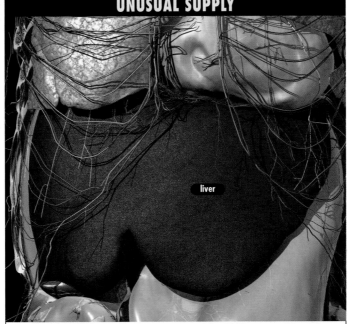

liver

One of the liver's main functions is to break down nutrients for the body. This means the liver has a unique blood supply.

- Most body parts are supplied with blood flowing along one or a few main arteries.

- The liver has a main artery, the *hepatic artery.*

- The liver also has a second and much greater blood supply.

- This comes along a vessel called the *hepatic portal vein.*

- The hepatic portal vein is the only main vein that does not take blood straight back to the heart.

- It runs from the intestines to the liver, bringing blood full of nutrients from digestion.

• See pages 36–37 for information on the BLOOD.

BABY LIVER

Most babies and young children have big abdomens. This is partly because their liver is much larger in proportion to the body's overall size, than the liver of an adult.

- An adult liver is usually $\frac{1}{40}$ of total body weight.

- A baby's liver is nearer $\frac{1}{20}$ of total body weight.

Babies and toddlers often have a tummy that sticks out, but it's not the stomach that causes this shape, it's their liver.

WHAT IS THE LIVER?

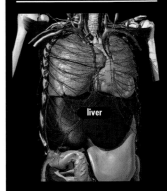

liver

The liver is the largest single organ inside the body.

- Wedge-shaped, dark red in color.

- Typical weight 3.3 lbs.

- Depth at widest part on right side 6 in.

- Has a larger right lobe and smaller left lobe.

- Lobes separated by a strong layer, the *falciform ligament.*

WHAT IS THE PANCREAS?

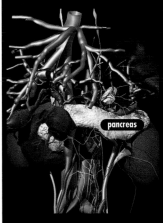

pancreas

The pancreas is a long, slim, wedge-shaped organ.

- It is soft, greyish-pink in color.

- Typical weight 3.5 oz.

- Typical length 6 in.

- Has three main parts: *head* (wide end), *body* (middle) and *tail* (tapering end).

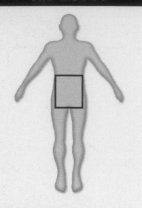

The parts of the urinary system are inside the lower body or abdomen. The kidneys are at the upper rear, on either side of the backbone behind the lower ribs. The bladder is the lowest part of the abdomen, between the hips.

KIDNEYS AND URINARY SYSTEM

Your body makes wastes and unwanted substances that it must remove. Some of this waste comes out of the end of the digestive tract and is called *solid waste*. The other main kind is liquid waste, called *urine*. Urine is created a very different way than solid waste. It is made, not from digestive leftovers, but by filtering the blood.

• *See pages 38–39 for information on DIGESTION.*

MAIN PARTS OF THE KIDNEY

Cortex
Outer layer, formed mainly of microscopic blood vessels from the filtering units, called *nephrons*.

Medulla
Inner layer, formed mainly from the tiny tubes of the nephrons.

Renal pelvis
Space in the middle of the kidney where urine collects.

KIDNEYS – SIZE AND SHAPE

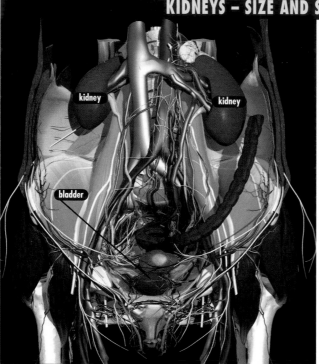

kidney

kidney

bladder

• The right kidney is usually about 0.4–0.6 in. lower than the left one.

• Each kidney is shaped like a bean with a slight indent on one side.

• Average kidney measurements are 4.3 in. high, 2.3 in. wide, and 1.1 in. from front to back.

• In a woman, the typical weight of the kidneys is 4.5–4.9 ounces.

• In a man, the typical weight is 4.9–5.2 ounces.

The kidneys' huge blood supply can be seen by the size of the renal arteries (red) and veins (blue). The pale ureter tubes lead down to the bladder.

KIDNEY MICROFILTERS

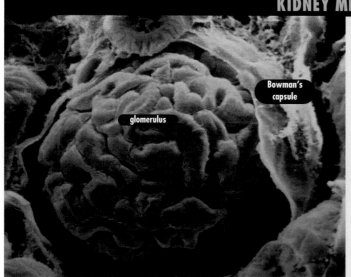

Bowman's capsule

glomerulus

Each kidney contains about one million microscopic filters, called *nephrons*.

• Each nephron begins with a tiny tangle or knot of the smallest blood vessels, called *capillaries*, known as the *glomerulus*.

• Waste substances and water squeeze out of the glomerulus into a cup-shaped part around it, called *Bowman's capsule*.

The work of the kidney takes place in the nephrons.

• The wastes and water then flow through a microscopic tube, the *renal tubule*, where some water, minerals, and salts are taken back into the blood.

• All the tiny tubules of all the nephrons in one kidney, straightened out and joined end to end, would stretch 62 miles.

• The end result is urine, which is mostly water containing dissolved wastes like urea and ammonia.

BLADDER – THE NEED TO GO

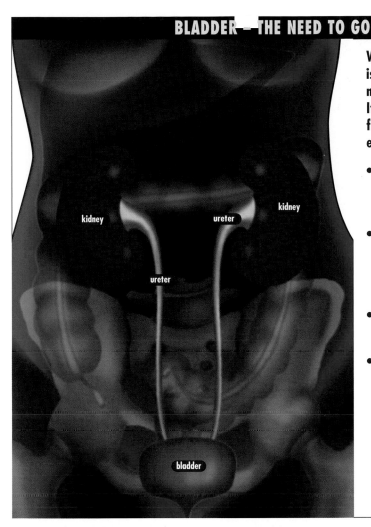

kidney

ureter

kidney

ureter

bladder

When empty, the bladder is pear-shaped and not much bigger than a thumb. It gradually stretches and fills with urine until it is emptied.

- We can tell how much urine is inside the bladder by how much we need to urinate.

- 8.4–10 fl. oz. of urine (about the amount in a coffee mug) – slight urge to release the urine by urination.

- 13.5–16.9 fl. oz. – stronger urge to urinate.

- 16.9–19.2 fl.oz. – desperate urge to urinate.

Bacteria can infect the bladder, causing *cystitis*. Symptoms include a burning sensation during urination and an urgent need to empty the bladder, although little urine comes out.

BLOOD TO URINE

The kidneys receive more blood, for their size, than any other body part.

Amount of blood
- Each minute at rest, the kidneys receive 2.5 pints of blood.

- This is about one-fifth of all the blood pumped out by the heart.

Quick flow
- This blood flows quickly through the kidneys, so they don't actually contain one-fifth of all the body's blood.

- Over 24 hours, all the blood in the body passes through the kidneys more than 300 times.

Amount of urine
- From this blood is filtered, on an average day, about 3 pints of urine.

Variation of amount
- However, the amount of urine varies according to how much water is taken into the body by food and drink.

- The amount of urine also varies according to how much water is lost in hot conditions as sweat.

Hot and cold
- On a hot day with few drinks, urine volume may be less than 2 pints.

- On a cold day with many drinks, urine volume may be more than 10.5 pints.

FEMALE AND MALE

- The urethra, which takes urine from the bladder to the outside, is different in females and males.

- This is because in males, the urethra is part of the reproductive system as well as the urinary system.

- In females, the urethra is 1.5 in. long and 0.23 in. across.

- In males it is 7 in. long and runs inside the penis.

Men and women have different systems for taking urine to the outside of the body.

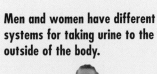

• See pages 48–49 for information on REPRODUCTION.

MAIN URINARY PARTS

Kidneys
Filter the blood to make waste liquid, known as *urine*.

Ureters
Tubes about 10–12 in. long that carry urine from the kidneys to the bladder.

Bladder
Correctly called the *urinary bladder*, it stores urine until it is "convenient" to get rid of it.

Urethra
Tube that carries urine from the bladder to the outside.

MEAT EATER

When you eat lots of meat, your urine gets darker. This is because your body makes urea, which gives urine its color, from protein.

• See pages 40–41 for information on the diet.

See pages 34–35 for information on the CIRCULATORY SYSTEM.

Genes, in the form of the chemical DNA, are present in almost all the microscopic cells in the body. Only a few cell types, like red blood cells, lack them.

Most children look like their parents. This is because parents pass on their genes to their children. Genes are instructions for how a human body grows, develops, maintains and repairs itself, and usually keeps itself healthy. Instructions for building a mechanical machine are usually written as words and drawn as diagrams. The genetic instructions for building and running the human body are in the form of a chemical substance, called *DNA*.

DNA

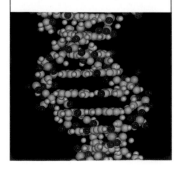

DNA is *deoxyribonucleic acid*. It is a chemical substance shaped like two ladders held and twisted like a corkscrew, called a *double helix*.

- DNA contains four kinds of chemical sub-units called bases, named *adenine* (A), *thymine* (T), *guanine* (G), and *cytosine* (C).

- Like words in a sentence, these bases are in a certain order along DNA.

- The order of the bases is the genetic code carrying the genetic instructions.

- In the full set of DNA there are 3,200 million sets of bases.

- This full set of DNA containing all the genes for the human body is called the *human genome*.

CHROMOSOMES

- There are 46 lengths of DNA in each cell's control center, called the *nucleus*.

- Each length is tightly wound into a shorter, thicker item, called a *chromosome*.

- The chromosomes are not all different, they are in 23 pairs.

- One chromosome from each pair came from the mother, and the other one from the father.

- Each time a cell divides as part of growth and normal body maintenance, all the chromosomes are copied.

- So each of the two resulting cells has the complete set of 23 pairs.

- All 46 pieces of DNA in the chromosomes from a single cell, straightened out and joined together, would stretch almost 6.5 feet.

- If the same was done to all the DNA in the body, it would stretch from the Earth to the Sun and back 100 times!

GENES IN LIVING THINGS

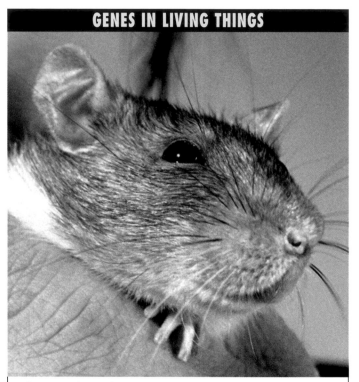

The genes that make a mouse are almost the same as those that make a person. Out of every 100 genes, a mouse has 92 that are the same as ours.

All human beings have the same overall set of genes. Tiny differences, in less than 1 out of 500 genes, make each of us unique.

- The exact number of genes that human beings is still disputed.

- Scientists believe human beings have somewhere between 30,000 and 35,000 genes.

- Nearly all other living things have genes formed of DNA, like human beings.

- Often, the same genes doing the same jobs occur in very different kinds of living things.

- The more similar living things are to us, the more similar the sets of genes.

- A chimp has 98 of every 100 genes in common with human beings.

- A fruit fly has 44 of every 100 genes in common with human beings.

STRONG AND WEAK GENES

- Each gene can exist in several forms, called *alleles*.

- The blue allele for the eye color gene tells the body how to make blue coloring substance for the iris.

- The brown allele tells the body how to make brown coloring substance for the iris.

- As mentioned above, each person has two copies of a gene, one inherited from the mother, one from the father.

- A person with two alleles for brown eyes has brown eyes.

- A person with two alleles for blue eyes has blue eyes.

- If a person has one allele for blue eyes and one for brown, the brown is stronger, called *dominant*, while the blue is weaker, called *recessive*, and the person has brown eyes.

- Many genes work in this way, with different alleles, which are dominant or recessive when put together.

In any family, the children usually look like at least one of their parents. Sometimes, children look more like their grandparents, because some characteristics do not show up in every generation.

• See page 49 for information on making eggs and sperm.

• See page 49 for information on making eggs and sperm.

WHAT ARE GENES?

A gene is a portion of DNA containing the chemical code for making a part of the body or instructing how that part works.

For example, the gene for eye color tells the body how to make the colored substance, called *pigment*, for the iris.

Number
- The human body has a total of about 30,000 genes.

- Sometimes, several genes work together to control one feature.

Instructions for appearance
Genes contain the information for skin color, hair color and type, overall adult height, ear lobe shape, and many other features of the body.

Instructions for processes
Genes also control how the body's chemical processes, like digesting food, work.

WHAT ARE CLONES?

Usually, each person has a unique selection of genes.

The exception is identical twins, who have exactly the same genes.

Living things with exactly the same genes are called *clones*.

Dolly the sheep is the most famous clone. Scientists took genes from an adult sheep and used them to create an identical copy.

GENETIC FINGERPRINTING

The DNA from skin, hair, and blood can help the police in their investigations. Genetic information can eliminate a suspect or help the police to secure a conviction.

Police procedures have been revolutionised since reliable DNA fingerprinting has been available.

- Small pieces of DNA, for example, from the white blood cells in a tiny speck of blood, can be copied millions of times.

- This is done by a laboratory process, called *polymerase chain reaction*, PCR.

- PCR gives enough DNA for testing to look at various sets or sequences of genes.

- The main testing method is called *gel electrophoresis*.

- The results are flat layers of a jelly-like substance containing dark bands, like a bar code.

- The sequence of bands gives a "genetic fingerprint."

- If two samples of DNA match exactly, the chances are millions to one that they came from the same body.

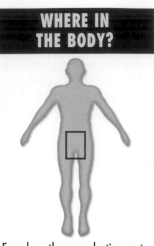
REPRODUCTION

All living things create more of their kind by breeding, called *reproduction*. The process of reproduction happens in the same basic way in the human body as it does in other animals, like cats, dogs, horses, mice, and whales. Sperm from a male is needed to fertilize the egg in a female, which then begins to grow into a new baby. The body parts that do this are called the *reproductive system*.

Female — the reproductive parts or sex organs are near the base of the lower body (abdomen).

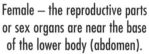

WHERE IN THE BODY?

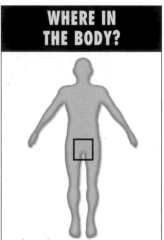

Male — the reproductive parts or sex organs are mostly below the abdomen, between the legs.

FEMALE PARTS

Ovaries
About 28 days, one egg cell is released as a ripe egg, or *ovum*.

Oviducts
Also called *fallopian tubes*. These carry the ripe egg toward the uterus.

Uterus (womb)
Where the new baby grows and develops from a fertilized egg during pregnancy.

Cervix
This is the neck of the womb. It stays closed during pregnancy, then opens at birth to allow the baby to be born.

Vagina (birth canal)
The new baby passes along this from the womb to the outside world at birth.

EGG CELLS

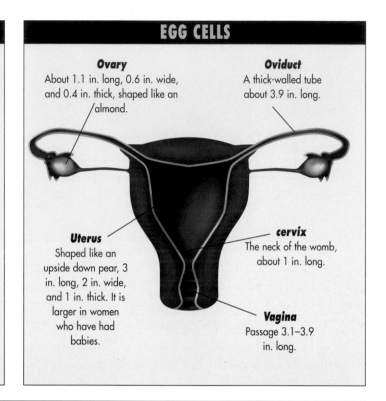

Ovary
About 1.1 in. long, 0.6 in. wide, and 0.4 in. thick, shaped like an almond.

Oviduct
A thick-walled tube about 3.9 in. long.

Uterus
Shaped like an upside down pear, 3 in. long, 2 in. wide, and 1 in. thick. It is larger in women who have had babies.

cervix
The neck of the womb, about 1 in. long.

Vagina
Passage 3.1–3.9 in. long.

EGG RELEASE CYCLE

day 1
start of period

day 17–20
fertilized egg implants into lining of womb

day 14
egg released into oviduct

day 14–16
egg fertilized by sperm

The menstrual cycle lasts about 28 days. The cycle first begins when a girl is about 10 to 14 years old.

- Once every 28 days or so, an egg cell ripens and is released from its ovary into the oviduct.

- This process is called *ovulation*.

- As it happens, the womb lining has become thick and rich with blood, ready to nourish the egg cell if it joins with a sperm cell and begins to develop into a baby.

- If this does not happen, the womb lining breaks down and is lost through the vagina as menstrual bleeding, called a *period*.

- Then, the whole process of egg ripening and uterus changes starts again.

- It is controlled mainly by hormones called *sex hormones*, *estrogen* and *progesterone*.

- See pages 50–51
STAGES OF LIFE

- See page 53 for information on HORMONES.

SPERM CELLS

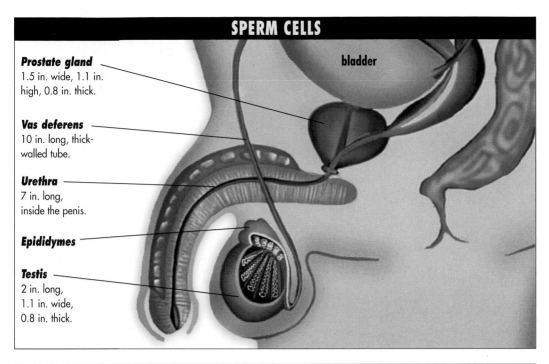

Prostate gland
1.5 in. wide, 1.1 in. high, 0.8 in. thick.

Vas deferens
10 in. long, thick-walled tube.

Urethra
7 in. long, inside the penis.

Epididymes

Testis
2 in. long, 1.1 in. wide, 0.8 in. thick.

bladder

MALE PARTS

Penis
Contains the urethra tube that sperm passes through as they leave the body, called *ejaculation*.

Testes
Make millions of microscopic sperm cells every day.

Vas deferens
Also known as the *ductus deferens*. Carry sperm cells from the testes and epididymes on their way out of the body.

Epididymes
Store sperm cells until they are released.

Scrotum
Bag of skin containing the testes and epididymes.

Prostate gland
Makes nourishing fluid for the sperm cells.

MAKING EGGS AND SPERM

When the body makes eggs or sperm, cells are copied in a unique way.

• Ordinary body cells divide into two to form more cells for growth, body maintenance, and repair.

• During this process all the genes in all the 23 pairs of chromosomes are copied, so each resulting cell receives a full set of 23 pairs.

• This type of cell division is called *mitosis*.

• Egg and sperm cells are made by a different type of cell division, called *meiosis*.

• In meiosis, the genes are not copied.

• Each egg or sperm receives just one of each pair of chromosomes, making 23 instead of 46.

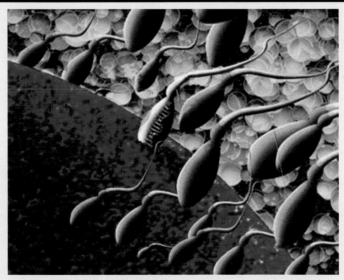

• When an egg joins with a sperm to create a new baby, the two sets of 23 chromosomes come together to form 23 pairs, which is back to the normal number.

• See pages 46–47 for information on GENES.

Genes are carried by sperm and eggs. Each carries half of the genetic material needed to form a new baby. When they meet, the halves join together to make a new individual.

FEMALE EGGS

Egg cells are about 0.1 mm across, almost microscopic.

• At birth a new baby girl has half a million unripe egg cells in her ovaries. The number decreases as she gets older.

• By the time a girl has grown up and is ready to have children, the number of egg cells in her body is about 200,000.

• Over the years when she can have children, a woman 's ovaries release about 400 egg cells.

MALE SPERM

Sperm are shaped like tiny tadpoles, with a rounded head and long tail.

• Among the smallest cells in the body, just 0.001 in. in total length.

• Tens of millions are made every day in a massive tangle of tubes in the testis, called *seminiferous tubules*.

• All the tubules from one testis straightened out and joined end to end would stretch over 109 yd.

• Each sperm cell takes about two months to form.

• Sperm is stored in the epididymis tube, which is folded and coiled next to the testis.

• Stretched out straight, the epididymis tube would stretch 20 feet.

• When sperm are released, about 200-500 million pass in fluid along the vas deferens and urethra, and out of the end of the penis.

• If they are not released, they break down and their parts are recycled within the body.

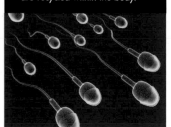

The development of a baby inside the mother's womb is called pregnancy and lasts about 9 months (average 266 days from fertilization to birth).

GROWTH RATES

Growth is fastest during early weeks in the womb and slows down towards birth.

- Speeds up slightly in first 2–3 years after birth.
- Slows down toward the end of childhood.
- Sudden spurt during puberty, usually early teens.
- Slows down towards late teens.
- Full height usually by 20 years old.

STAGES OF LIFE

Every human body starts as a fertilized egg cell, a tiny speck smaller than the dot on this **i**. By the process of cell division, that single cell becomes two, four, eight, and so on, building the human body. About 20 years later, by the time of adulthood, the body has 10 trillion cells of more than 200 different kinds. It is a fascinating story of amazing growth and development.

IN THE WOMB: WEEK ONE

Egg cell is joined or fertilized by sperm cell, usually in the oviduct of the mother. The genes of egg and sperm (in the form of DNA) come together and the genetic blueprint for a new body is formed.

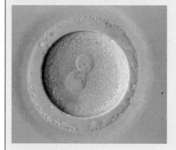

24-36 hours
Fertilized egg cell splits into two smaller cells.

36-48 hours
Each of the two cells divide, forming four cells.

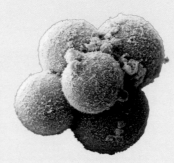

2-3 days
Cell division continues, forming a tiny ball of more than a 20 cells moving slowly along the oviduct.

4 days
The ball of more than 100 cells, called a *morula*, reaches the inside of the uterus.

5 days
The ball of hundreds of cells becomes hollow inside, called a *blastocyst* (early embryo).

6-7 days

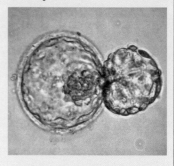

The blastocyst, still only 0.003–0.007 in. across, implants into the blood-rich lining of the uterus.

The cells now take in nourishment from the lining and enlarge between divisions.

IN THE WOMB: EMBRYO

For the first 8 weeks after fertilization, the developing baby is called an *embryo*.

Week 2
The embryo becomes the shape of a flat disc, surrounded by fluid, within the uterus lining. The disc lengthens and curls over at the edges.

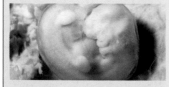

Week 3
The curled-over disc becomes longer and larger at one end and begins the shape of the head and brain. Length is about 0.06 in.

Week 4

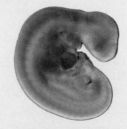

The embryo becomes C-shaped. Simple tubes start to make the heart and begin pulsating. Arms and legs begin as small bulges on the body. Length is about 0.2 in.

Week 5
Head and brain grow rapidly. Inner organs begin to fomr. Nose begins to take shape. Length is about 0.31 in.

Week 6

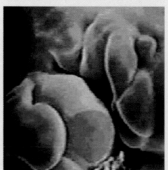

Heart and lungs almost formed, body becomes straighter. Eyes and ears obvious. Length is about 0.47 in.

Week 7
Fingers and toes start to take shape. Neck becomes more visible. Tail shrinks. Length is about 0.6 in.

Week 8

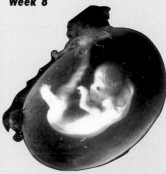

Muscles and eyelids form, and the tail has almost disappeared. All main body parts are present, even eyelids. Length is about 0.67 in.

This picture shows the embryo floating in its amniotic bag of fluid.

IN THE WOMB: FETUS

For the period between 8 weeks after fertilization and birth, the developing baby is called a *fetus*.

Month 3
Finishing touches developed, including folds for fingernails and toenails. Eyelids closed. Head still very large compared to body. Length 1.5 in.

Month 4
Face looks much more human, first hair grows on head. First bones begin to harden. Length 2.1 in.

Month 5
Reproductive parts begin to take shape, showing if the fetus is a girl or body. Length 6 in.

Month 6
Body becomes slimmer and is covered with fine hair, called *lanugo*. Fetus can move arms and kick legs.

Month 7
Body is lean and wrinkled. Fetus can swallow, eyes can detect light.

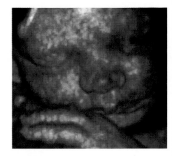

Month 8
Body puts on fat. Nails grow to ends of fingers and toes.

Month 9
Baby is chubbier and fully formed. Average weight at birth is 7.7–8.8 lbs. Average length is 20–24 in.

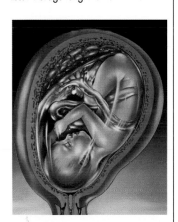

NEW BABY

By their first birthday, most babies have almost tripled their birth weight, from just over 7 to almost 22 lbs. They have also grown in height from about 21.6–30 in. Average times for movement and coordination skills (although there are wide variations)

4-8 weeks
Smiles in response to faces.
2-4 months
Raises head and shoulders when lying on stomach.
5-7 months
Rolls over from stomach to back.
6-8 months
Sits up perhaps with help, starts to make babbling noises.
7-9 months
Begins to try and feed itself, puts items in mouth.
8-10 months
Crawls.
10-12 months
Stands up with support.
12-15 months
Walks unaided.

Most people are at peak physical fitness from early-20s to mid-30s.

- Most men run their lifetime best between 27 and 29 years old.
- Most women run their lifetime best between 29 and 31 years old.
- Most marathon runners perform their best between 30 and 37 years old.

Certain reactions and body processes begin to slow down from the 40s in some people, but not until the 60s in others.

Signs of aging:
- *Wrinkled skin*
- *Graying or whitening of hair*
- *Hair loss*
- *Less muscle power*
- *More brittle bones*
- *Less flexible joints*
- *Senses become weaker*
- *The first sense to deteriorate is usually hearing, followed by sight. Touch and taste also become weaker, and then smell.*

PUBERTY

Puberty is the time when the body grows and develops rapidly from girl to woman or boy to man, and the reproductive (sex) parts start to work.

Puberty - girls
- Can occur any time between 9 and 16 years of age. It usually lasts 2–3 years.
- First signs include rapid growth and breasts begin to enlarge.
- Hair grows under arms and between legs, called *pubic hair*.
- Hips increase in width.
- Pads of fat laid down under skin give more rounded body outline.
- Voice deepens slightly.
- Menstrual cycle begins with first period, called *menarche*.

Puberty - boys
- Can occur any time between 11 and 17 years of age. It usually takes 3–4 years.
- First signs include rapid growth in height and hair growing under arms, between legs, and on face (moustache and beard).
- Shoulders increase in width.
- Muscle development increases giving more angular body outline.
- Voice deepens considerably or "breaks."
- Reproductive organs enlarge and begin to make sperm.

HORMONES

WHERE IN THE BODY?

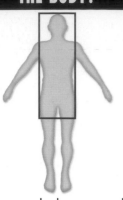

Hormone glands are scattered through the central body, from the head down through the neck into the lower abdomen. The reproductive organs, the ovaries in women and the testes in men, are also hormonal glands.

Your brain controls your body. It tells muscles to pull, the lung to breathe and the heart to beat. It does this by sending out tiny electrical signals, called *nerve messages*. But the brain also controls certain processes in another way, through natural body chemicals, called *hormones*. These are made in hormone or endocrine glands. The hormones travel around the body in the blood and affect how your body works. When you are frightened and your heart pounds, that's a hormone at work, called *adrenaline*.

THYROID

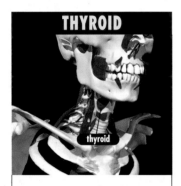

thyroid

Where
Under the skin of the neck just below the voicebox, wrapped around the upper windpipe.

Shape
Like a bowtie or butterfly.

Size
3.1–3.9 in. wide, 1.1 in. high, 0.8 in. thick, and weighs 0.8 lbs.

Hormones made
Thyroxine (T4), tri-iodothyronine (T3), and calcitonin

Effects
T4 and T3 make all the body's cells work faster so the whole body chemistry, or *metabolism*, speeds up. Calcitonin lowers the level of the mineral *calcium* in the blood.

PARATHYROIDS

Where
4 glands, two embedded in each side of the thyroid.

Shape
Like tiny eggs.

Size
Each are 0.22 in. high, 0.15 in. wide, 0.08 in. thick, and weighs 0.0001 lbs.

Hormones made
Parathormone

Effects
Controls the level of calcium in blood.

Calcium is vital for our brains, muscles, and blood to work properly, as well as building bones.

• See page 40 for information on calcium.

PITUITARY

The pituitary gland helps children to grow properly. It is sometimes called the *master gland,* because it controls several other glands.

One of the smallest hormone glands, but the most important. It is controlled by the brain and sends out hormones that affect the workings of other hormonal glands.

Where
Behind the eyes and below the central front of the brain, joined to it by a narrow stalk.

Shape
Bean-like.

Size
0.4 in. high, 0.47 in. wide, 0.3 in. thick, and weighs 0.017 lbs.

Hormones made
About 10 including GH (growth hormone), ADH (antidiuretic hormone), and TSH (thyroid-stimulating hormone).

Effects
GH makes the whole body increase in size and development.

• ADH makes the kidneys take back more water as they form urine.

• TSH makes the thyroid gland release more of its own hormones.

• See pages 44–45 for information on the KIDNEYS

PANCREAS

Where
In the upper left abdomen, behind the stomach.

Shape
Long, slim wedge-shaped.

Size
6 in. long, weighs about 3.5 oz.

Hormones made
Insulin and glucagon, made in about one million tiny cells, called *islets*, scattered through the pancreas.

Effects
Insulin lowers level of glucose by making body cells take in more of it. Glucagon raises the level.

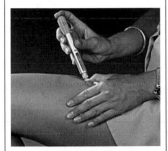

People with diabetes have a problem with the hormone *insulin*. They may have to inject insulin into their bodies.

• See page 43 for information on the role the pancreas plays in digestion.

THYMUS

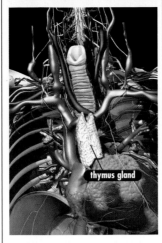
thymus gland

The thymus gland in the chest helps to make the white blood cells which destroy germs.

Where
Behind the breastbone.

Shape
Two joined sausage-like lobes.

Size
Relatively large in young children, thumb-sized and weighing up to 0.7 oz., shrinks slightly during adulthood.

Hormones made
Thymosin, thymopoietin, and others

Effects
Helps white blood cells to develop their germ-attacking powers.

• See pages 36–37 for information on the BLOOD.

ADRENALS

Where
2 glands, one above each kidney.

Shape
Like a small pyramid on the kidney.

Size
Each is 2 in. high, 1.1 in. wide, 0.4 in. thick, and weighs 0.17 oz.

Hormones made
Outer part, called the *cortex*, makes *corticosteroid*, or steroid hormones, including *cortisol* and *aldosterone*; inner part, called the *medulla*, makes adrenaline and similar hormones.

Effects
Cortisol decreases the effects of stress and helps control blood sugar and body repair, aldosterone affects how the kidneys filter blood.

See the box on the right for information on adrenaline.

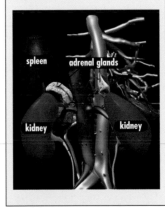
spleen   adrenal glands
kidney   kidney

FIGHT OR FLIGHT?

When the body is stressed or frightened and has to act fast, the adrenal glands releases their hormone *adrenaline*, also called *epinephrine*.

This helps it to get ready to face a threat and *fight*, or escape and flee from the danger in *flight*. The main effects of adrenaline are:

Blood vessels
• Widens blood vessels to muscles and heart muscle.

Heart
• Increases heart rate.
• Increases amount of blood pumped by each heartbeat.

Breathing
• Increases breathing rate.
• Widens airways in lungs allowing more air with each breath.

Digestion
• Decreases activity of inner organs. like stomach and intestines.

Sugar levels
• Raises level of glucose to provide more energy for muscles.

Our ancestors would have had to act fast if they saw a potentially dangerous predator. Adrenaline prepared the body for the responses they would have made.

OTHER HORMONE-MAKING PARTS

small intestine

Some body parts make hormones in addition to their main tasks.

Stomach
Gastrin makes stomach lining release acid.

Heart
Atriopeptin affects amounts of body salts and minerals and blood pressure.

Testes
Testosterone gives men their male characteristics.

Ovaries
Estrogen and progesterone give women their female characteristics.

• See pages 48–49 REPRODUCTION.

The small intestine makes the hormone *secretin*, which tells the pancreas to release acid-neutralizing juices.

53

LYMPH AND IMMUNE SYSTEMS

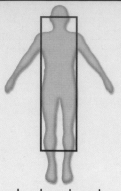

Lymph nodes and vessels are found in most body parts, especially in the neck, armpits, chest, central abdomen, and groin. They are also in the adenoids at the rear of the nasal chamber, the tonsils in the throat, the spleen behind the left kidney, and the thymus gland behind the breastbone.

When people are ill, their glands often swell, especially in the neck, armpits, and groin. But these are not really glands. They are called *lymph nodes*, and they are part of the lymphatic system. This system is the body's alternative circulation method. Like blood, lymph fluid flows around the body in tubes, called *lymph vessels*. Also like blood, it carries nutrients to many parts and collects waste. It is closely linked to the immune system, which specializes in attacking germs and fighting disease.

LYMPH NODES

There are about 500 lymph nodes all over the body.

- The larger ones are in the neck, armpits, chest, central abdomen and groin. There are others in the crook of the elbow and the back of the knee.
- Most are shaped like balls, beans, or pears.
- Smallest ones less than 0.04 in. across, larger ones 0.6–.78 in.
- Contain mainly various kinds of white blood cells.
- Can double in size when fighting illness.
- Lymph flows into each along several afferent lymph vessels.
- Lymph flows away from each along one efferent vessel.

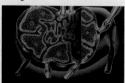

A typical lymph node contains lymph fluid and white blood cells.

LYMPH FLUID

Lymph fluid is usually pale or milky in colour.

- The average amount in the human body is 2–4.2 fl.oz.
- Contains mainly water, dissolved nutrients, and disease-fighting white blood cells and the antibodies they make.
- Forms from fluid that oozes out of and between cells and collects inside and between tissues.
- Flows slowly along smaller lymph vessels, which join to form larger ones.
- The fluid has no pump of its own but moves by general body pressure and the massaging effect of muscles and movements.
- Flows through lymph nodes on its journey.
- Lymph network gradually gathers lymph into two main lymph vessels of ducts in the chest.
- These are the *right lymphatic duct* and the *thoracic duct*.
- These ducts join the right and left subclavian veins where lymph joins the blood.

SPECIALIST LYMPH PARTS

Adenoids
- Also called *pharyngeal tonsils.*
- Found at the rear of the nasal chamber in the uppermost throat.
- Consist of a gathering of small lymph nodes, called *nodules.*
- Help to kill germs in air breathed.
- Swell up when battling illness, causing problems with air flow through the nose, and may need removal if this happens too often.

Tonsils

Red, sore, swollen tonsils are a sign of tonsillitis.

- Also called *palatine tonsils.*
- Found at the sides of the throat, just below and on either side of the soft palate (rear of the roof of the mouth).
- Consist of a gathering of small lymph nodes, called *nodules.*

- Help to kill germs in air breathed, food, and drink.
- Swell up when battling illness, causing a sore throat.
- Tonsils may need removal if this happens too often.

Spleen

spleen

The dark-red spleen stores blood, recycles old red blood cells, and makes new white cells.

- Behind and above the left kidney.
- Largest collection of lymph tissue in the body.
- Length about 4.7 in. (the size of a clenched fist).
- Weight about 5.2 oz., but can be half or twice this according to blood content and body's state of health.

• *See page 30–31 for information on the airways.*

IMMUNE SYSTEM

When we catch a cold, our immune system begins fighting it immediately. Colds usually last only a few days.

The immune system involves the lymph and blood systems and also many other body parts.

- Based on white blood cells of various kinds.

- Defends against harmful substances, like toxins or poisons.

- Also protects the body against invasion by germs such as bacteria, viruses and microscopic parasites, called *protists* or *protozoans*.

- Helps to clean away debris from normal body maintenance, as old cells die and break down.

IMMUNITY

Once we have caught an illness and fought the infection, we have immunity to the germ in the future.

- After the body catches an infection, especially by a virus germ, white cells, called *memory cells,* "remember" the type of virus.

- If the germ invades again later, the immune system can recognize and fight it right away and usually defeat it quickly.

- This is called *being resistant* or *immune* to that particular germ.

Viruses and bacteria are contagious, which means they spread between people.

TYPES OF IMMUNITY

The body becomes immune to illnesses in several ways.

Innate or native immunity
Already in the body.

Acquired immunity
Occurs after exposure to antigens, for example, on the surface of a type of germ.

Natural acquired immunity
Happens when the body catches the germ naturally.

Artificial acquired immunity
When an altered form of the germ or its products is put into the body specifically by vaccination.

Active immunity
When the body makes its own antigens.

Passive immunity
When ready-made antibodies are put into the body.

We are exposed to many germs in our every day life. As we grow up, our bodies gain immunity to most of germs naturally. There are only a few diseases we need to be protected from artificially, through immunizations.

MAIN DEFENDERS – LYMPHOCYTES

Lymphocytes are one of the main kinds of white blood cells.

The healthy body contains about 2 trillion lymphocytes. They are made in bone marrow. There are two main kinds, B-cells and T-cells.

T-cell lymphocytes
- T-cell lymphocytes are processed or 'trained' in the thymus gland.

- T-cell lymphocytes kill "foreign" invading cells, like bacteria.

- T-cell lymphocytes also encourage B-cells to make antibodies.

- T-cell lymphocytes also encourage white cells, called *macrophages*, to engulf invading microbes.

B-cell lymphocytes
- B-cell lymphocytes respond the chemical messages from T-cell lymphocytes.

- B-cell lymphocytes are encouraged into activity by T-cells.

- B-cells change into plasma cells which make defensive substances, called *antibodies.*

- Different antibodies are made in response to different antigens, which are "foreign" substances on various invading microbes or made by them.

- Antibodies travel in the blood and lymph fluid.

- Antibodies join to antigens and destroy them.

• See page 16 for information on BONE MARROW and page 36–37 for information on BLOOD.

55

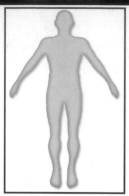

Any part of the body has the potential to stop functioning as well as it should.

DISEASES AND MEDICINES

Most of the time, human beings are well. Nearly everyone gets the occasional cold and cough. Some people have a few bigger health problems, like an infection, such as chickenpox, or an injury, such as a sprained joint or broken bone. A few people are ill quite often. However, the basic rules for good health are the same: do not smoke, eat a nutritious and balanced diet, get plenty of exercise and activity, and keep a positive attitude.

TYPES OF MEDICINES

Anaesthetic
Reduces or gets rid of sensations, including pain.

Analgesic
Reduces pain.

Beta-blocker
Slows heartbeat and makes it more regular, lowers blood pressure.

Bronchodilator
Widens, or *dilates*, the small airways, called *bronchioles*, in the lungs.

Cytotoxic
Destroys cells, especially malignant or cancerous ones, in chemotherapy.

Diuretic
Reduces water content of the body by increasing amount of urine.

Immunosuppressive
Reduces the actions of the body's immune defense system. For example, so it does not reject an organ transplanted from another person.

Steriods
Large group of medicines, including hormones and substances, that help to increase muscle size or reduce the action of the immune defense system.

Thrombolytic
Dissolves blood clots.

Vasoconstrictor
Makes the small artery blood vessels narrower.

Vasodilator
Makes the small artery blood vessels wider.

MEDICAL DRUGS

Many drugs have a name that begins *anti-*. This shows which problem the drug fights against.

Antibiotic
Disables or destroys microbes, mainly bacteria.

Anticoagluant
Prevents blood clotting.

Anticonvulsant
Lessens the risk of convulsions or seizures.

Antidepressant
Reduces the effects of depressive illness by lifting mood.

Antiemetic
Reduces feelings of sickness or nausea.

Antifungal
Disables or destroys fungal microbes.

Antihistamine
Used against allergic-type illnesses such as hay fever, asthma, and food allergy.

Anti-inflammatory
Reducing inflammation (redness, swelling, soreness, and pain)

Antipyretic
Lowers fever, reduces body temperature.

Antiseptic
Kills most kinds of germs, usually applied to the skin.

Antitoxin
Makes a poisonous or toxic substance harmless.

Antiviral
Disables or destroys virus microbes.

MAJOR CAUSES OF ILLNESS AND DISEASE

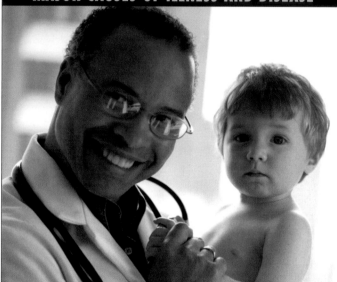

The symptoms of an illness are usually easy to tell, but it can be quite hard for doctors to diagnose the cause of a problem.

- Genetic problems that can be passed on from parents or begin as a new case when genes are not copied correctly as cells multiply in the developing body.

- Congenital problems that are present at birth.

- Infections caused by invading microbes.

- Infestations due to worms, fleas, and similar animals.

- Malnutrition, due to not enough food and/or foods which are not balanced in their nutrients.

- Toxins or poisons from the surroundings, such as in water.

- Physical harm by accidents and injuries.

- Radiation, such as radioactivity, nuclear rays, and the sun's harmful ultraviolet rays.

- Cancers, where cells multiply out of control and spread to invade other body parts.

- Autoimmune problems, where the body's immune defence system mistakenly attacks the body (as in rheumatoid arthritis).

- Allergic disorders, where the body's immune defence system mistakenly attacks harmless substances, like plant pollen in hay fever.

- Metabolic conditions, when there is a problem with the inner processes of body chemistry.

BACTERIA

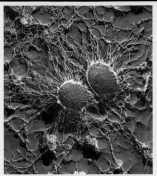

Two bacteria, magnified 50,000 times.

- Each bacteria is a single cell.

- Microscopic, about 100,000 would fit inside this letter *o*.

- Different groups are known by their shapes, such as *cocci* (balls or spheres), *bacilli* (rods or sausages), and *spirochaetes* (corkscrews).

- Many are disabled or killed by antibiotic drugs.

- Bacterial infections include many kinds of sore throat, skin boils, pertussis (whooping cough), tetanus, scarlet fever, most kinds of cholera and dysentery, plague, diphtheria, Legionnaire's disease, many kinds of bronchitis, most types of food poisoning, ear infections, and anthrax.

MICROFUNGI

- Each microfungi is a single cell.

- Belong to the fungus group, which includes mushrooms, toadstools, and yeasts.

- Often grow and spread on the skin.

- Diseases include athlete's foot, ringworm, and fungal nail and hair infections.

PROTISTS (PROTOZOA)

The disease *malaria* is caused by a protist. It is transmitted to humans through mosquitos.

- Each protist is a single cell.

- Sometimes called *parasites* or *microparasites*.

- Most are microscopic, about 1,000 would fit inside this *o*.

- More common in warmer countries.

- Diseases caused include malaria (plasmodium), sleeping sickness (trypanosome), Chagas' disease (trypanosoma cruzi), and river blindness (schistosomiasis).

VIRUSES

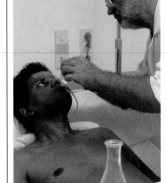

Scientists can only treat the symptoms of most viral infections, not the virus itself.

- Smallest known forms of life, often considered living and nonliving things.

- About half a million would fit on this period.

- Invade the body's own microscopic cells.

- Take over these cells and make them produce more copies of the virus.

- Viral infections include common colds, most types of flu (influenza), polio (poliomyelitis), skin warts, chickenpox, measles, mumps, rubella, yellow fever, most kinds of hepatitis, rabies, Ebola, and AIDS (due to Human Immunodeficiency Virus, HIV).

- Are not affected by antibiotic drugs.

- Several viral infections can be prevented by vaccination to make the body resistant or immune to them, called *immunization*.

• *See page 55 for information on TYPES OF IMMUNITY.*

DISEASE-CAUSING MICROBES

- Several kinds of harmful microbes cause infectious diseases, or *infections*.

- They are known commonly as *germs*.

- Most get into the body through air, in food or drink, or through wounds.

- When a harmful microbe spreads by direct or personal contact between people, rather than by indirect means, such as air or water, this is known as a *contagious infection*.

- The time when the harmful microbe multiplies inside the body, but the person does not show signs of illness, is the incubation period.

MEDICAL SPECIALISTS

Anaesthetist
Giving anaesthetics to remove sensation and pain while patient is still conscious (local anaesthetic) or to make the patient unconscious as well (general anaesthetic).

Cardiologist
Heart and main blood vessels.

Dermatologist
Skin, hair, and nails.

Gynecologist
Female reproductive and urinary organs.

Geriatrics
Old age and old age diseases.

Haematologist
Blood and body fluids.

Neurologist
Brain and nerves.

Obstetrician
Pregnancy and birth.

Oncologist
Tumours, especially cancers and similar conditions.

Ophthalmologist
Eyes.

Orthopaedic surgeon
Bones, joints, and the skeleton.

Paediatrician
Care of children.

Pathologist
The processes and changes of disease, such as laboratory studies of samples.

Physiotherapist
Using physical measures such as massage, manipulation, exercise, and heat.

Primary Care Physician
General family heathcare.

Psychiatrist
Mental and behavioral problems.

Radiologist
Diagnoses with X-rays and scans.

Thoracic surgeon
Chest, especially lungs and airways, also heart.

Urologist
Urinary system of kidneys, bladder, and their tubes.

GLOSSARY

Abdomen The lower part of the main body or torso, below the chest, that mainly contains digestive and excretory organs, and in females, reproductive parts.

Artery A blood vessel that conveys blood away from the heart.

Axon The very long, thin part of a nerve cell or neuron, also called a *nerve fiber*.

Bladder Bag-like sac or container for storing fluids. The body has several, including the urinary bladder, often just called *the bladder*, and gall bladder.

Blood sugar Also called *glucose*, the body's main energy source, used by all its microscopic cells to carry out their life processes and functions.

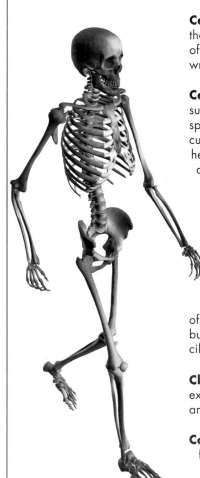

Capillary The smallest type of blood vessels, usually less than 0.02 in. long and too thin to see except through a microscope.

Cardiac Having to do with the heart.

Cartilage Tough, light, slightly bendy and compressible body substance, often called *gristle*, that forms parts of the skeleton, such as the ears and nose, and also covers the ends of bones in joints.

Cell The basic microscopic "building block" of the body, a single living unit, with most cells being 1/1,000 in. across. The body contains over 10 trillion cells.

Central nervous system The brain and spinal cord.

Cerebral Having to do with the cerebrum, the largest part of the brain that forms its wrinkled domed shape.

Cerebrospinal fluid Liquid surrounding the brain and spinal cord, to protect and cushion them as well as helping provide nourishment and taking away waste.

Cilium Microscopic hair, usually sticking out from the surface of a cell, that can wave or bend, and perhaps sense substances, such as the olfactory epithelium of the nose and in the taste buds on the tongue. (Plural: cilia.)

Clone A living thing with exactly the same genes as another living thing.

Collagen Tiny, tough, strong fibers found in body parts such as skin and bones.

Cortex The outer part or layer of a body part, such as the renal cortex of the kidney or the cerebral cortex of the brain.

Cranium The upper domed part of the skull that covers and protects the brain.

Cermis The inner layer of skin, under the **epidermis**, that contains the touch sensors, hair follicles, and sweat glands.

DNA Deoxyribonucleic acid, the chemical substance that forms the genetic information, called *genes*.

Embryo The name for a developing human body, from fertilization as a single cell to eight weeks later.

Endocrine Having to do with hormones and the hormonal system (*see* **hormone**).

Enzymes Substances that alter the speed of a chemical change or reaction, usually speeding it up, but remain unchanged themselves at the end of the reaction.

Epidermis The protective outer layer of skin, which is always being worn away but continually replacing itself.

Excretory Having to do with removing waste substances from the body. The main excretory system is made up of the kidneys, bladder and their linking tubes.

Fertilization When an egg cell joins a sperm cell to start the development of a new human body.

Fetus A developing human body, from eight weeks after fertilization until birth.

Fovea The small area in the retina of the eye where vision is most detailed and clearest, due to the large number of cone cells.

Gastric Having to do with the stomach.

Gland A body part that makes a substance that it then releases, such as the tear glands that make tear fluid for the eyes, and the sweat glands in the skin.

Glucose *See* **blood sugar**.

Gustatory Having to do with the tongue and taste.

Hepatic Having to do with the liver.

Hormone A natural chemical messenger that circulates in the blood and affects how certain body parts work, helping the nervous system to control and coordinate all body processes.

Humor Old word used to describe various body fluids, still used in some cases. For example, to describe the fluids inside the eye, the vitreous humor and aqueous humor.

Immunity Protection or resistance to microbial germs and other harmful substances.

Integumentary Having to do with the skin and other coverings, including nails and hair.

Ligament A stretchy, strap-like part that joins the bones around a joint, so the bones do not move too far apart.

Medulla The central region of a body part, such as the renal medulla of the kidney, or the adrenal medulla of the adrenal gland.

Meninges Three thin layers covering the brain and spinal cord, and also making and containing cerebrospinal fluid. They are known as the *dura mater*, *arachnoid*, and *pia mater*.

Meiosis Part of special type of cell division, when the chromosomes are not copied and only one set (not a double-set) moves into each resulting cell.

Metabolism All of the body's thousands of chemical processes, changes, and reactions, such as breaking apart blood sugar to release energy, and building up amino acids into proteins.

Mineral A simple chemical substance, usually a metal such as iron or calcium, or a salt-type chemical, such as phosphate, which the body needs in small quantities from food to stay healthy.

Mitosis Part of normal cell division, when the chromosomes have been copied and one full double-set moves into each resulting cell.

Motor nerve A nerve that carries messages from the brain to a muscle, telling it when to contract, or to a gland, telling it when to release its content.

Mucus Thickish, sticky, slimy substance made by many body parts, often for protection and lubrication, such as inside the nose and within the stomach.

Myo- Having to do with muscles, such as myocardium or heart muscle.

Nephron Microscopic filtering unit in the kidney for cleaning the blood.

Neuron A nerve cell, the basic unit of the nervous system.

Olfactory Having to do with the nose and smell.

Optic Having to do with the eye, especially the optic nerve carrying messages from the eye to the brain.

Papillae Small bumps on a body part, such as the tongue.

Peripheral nerves The bodywide network of nerves, excluding the central nervous system.

Peristalsis Wave-like contractions of muscles in the wall of a body tube, such as the small intestine, ureter (from kidney to bladder), or oviduct (from ovary to womb).

Pulmonary Having to do with the lungs.

Renal Having to do with the kidneys.

Sebum Natural waxy substance, made in sebaceous glands associated with hair follicles, that keeps skin supple and fairly waterproof.

Sensory nerve A nerve that carries messages to the brain from a sense part, such as the eye, the ear, the tiny stretch sensors in muscles and joints, and the blood pressure sensors in main arteries.

Skeletal Having to do with the skeleton.

System In the body, a set of major parts and organs that all work together to fulfil one main task, such as the respiratory system, which transfers oxygen from the air around to the blood.

Tendon The string, fibrous, rope-like end of a muscle, where it tapers and joins to a bone.

Thoracic Having to do with the chest, called the *thorax*.

Thrombosis The process of blood going lumpy to form a clot, also known as a *thrombus*.

Tissue A group of very similar cells all doing the same job, such as muscle tissue, adipose, or fat tissue, epithelial (covering or lining) tissue, and connective tissue (joining and filling in gaps between other parts).

Valve A flap, pocket, or similar part that allows a substance to pass one way but not the other.

Vein A blood vessel that conveys blood toward the heart.

Vertebra A single bone of the row of bones called the *backbone*, *spine*, or *vertebral column*.

Villi Tiny finger-like objects from the microscopic cells in various body parts, including the inner lining of the small intestine.

Visceral Having to do with the main parts or organs inside the abdomen (the lower part of the torso), mainly the stomach, intestines, kidneys, bladder, and in females, reproductive parts.

Vitamin Substance needed in fairly small amounts from food for the body to work well and stay healthy.

INDEX

INDEX

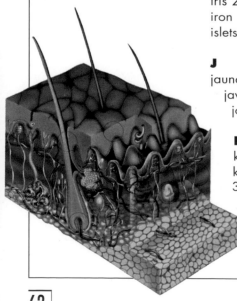

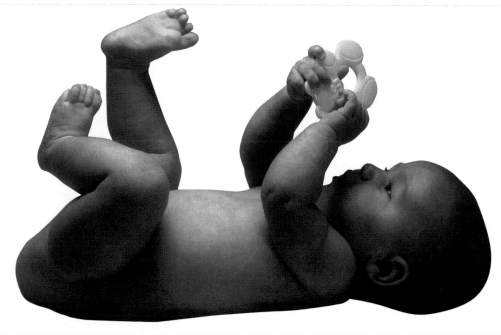